D0229784

BLOODAXE CONTEMPORARY FRENCH POETS

Throughout the twentieth century, France has been a dominant force in the development of European culture. It has made essential contributions and advances not just in literature but in all the arts, from the novel to film and philosophy; in drama (Theatre of the Absurd), art (Cubism and Surrealism) and literary theory (Structuralism and Post-Structuralism). These very different art forms and intellectual modes find a dynamic meeting-point in post-war French poetry.

Some French poets are absorbed by the latest developments in philosophy or psychoanalysis. Others explore relations between poetry and painting, between the written word and the visual image. There are some whose poetry is rooted in Catholicism, and others who have remained faithful to Surrealism, and whose poetry is bound to a life of action or political commitment.

Because it shows contemporary French poetry in a broader context, this new series will appeal both to poetry readers and to anyone with an interest in French culture and intellectual life. The books themselves also provide an imaginative and exciting approach to French poets which makes them ideal study texts for schools, colleges and universities.

Each volume is a single, unabridged collection of poems presented in a parallel-text format, with the French text facing an English verse translation by a distinguished expert or poet-translator. The editor of each book is an authority on the particular writer, and in each case the editor's introduction presents not only a critical appreciation of the work and its place in the author's output but also a comprehensive account of its social, intellectual and cultural background.

The series itself has been planned in such a way that the individual volumes will build up into a stimulating and informative introduction to contemporary French poetry, giving readers both an intimate experience of how French poets think and write, and a working overview of what makes poetry important in France.

BLOODAXE CONTEMPORARY FRENCH POETS

Series Editors: Timothy Mathews & Michael Worton

Keith Bosley has published a few collections of poems and many books of translation, mainly from French, Portuguese and Finnish poetry. His translations from French include *An Idiom of Night*, a selection from Pierre Jean Jouve (1968); the last Penguin Mallarmé (1977); and *From the Theorems of Master Jean de La Ceppède* (1983). A booklet of André Frénaud, *A Round O* (1977), was an early product of his friendship with the poet. His most recent collection of his own poetry is *A Chiltern Hundred* (Anvil Press, 1987).

Peter Broome is Professor of French at Queen's University, Belfast. He is co-author of *The Appreciation of Modern French Poetry* and of *An Anthology of Modern French Poetry* (Cambridge University Press, 1976), and author of monographs on Henri Michaux and on André Frénaud, as well as of studies of a variety of French writers, including André Gide. He wrote the introductory essay to Henri Michaux's *Spaced, Displaced* in the Bloodaxe Contemporary French Poets series, and is currently completing a major study of Baudelaire's *Les Fleurs du mal*.

Timothy Mathews is Professor of French at University College, London. He has published *Reading Apollinaire: Theories of Poetic Language* (Manchester University Press, 1987), and is completing a book for Cambridge University Press on alienation in modern French literature and painting. The first volume in the Bloodaxe Contemporary French Poets series, *On the Motion and Immobility of Douve* by Yves Bonnefoy, has an introduction by Timothy Mathews.

Michael Worton is Professor of French at University College London. He has published extensively on contemporary French writers, co-edited *Intertextuality: Theories and Practices* and *Textuality and Sexuality: Reading Theories and Practices* (Manchester University Press, 1990 and 1993), published two books on Michel Tournier, and is now writing a book on reading. The second volume in the Bloodaxe Contemporary French Poets series, *The Dawn Breakers* by René Char, is introduced and translated by Michael Worton.

For further details of the Bloodaxe Contemporary French Poets series, please see pages 8 and 119-24 of this book.

BLOODAXE CONTEMPORARY FRENCH POETS: 7

ANDRÉ FRÉNAUD

Rome the Sorceress

La Sorcière de Rome

Translated by
KEITH BOSLEY

Introduction by
PETER BROOME

BLOODAXE BOOKS

BLOODAXE CONTEMPORARY FRENCH POETS: 7
André Frénaud: *Rome the Sorceress*

Original French text of *La Sorcière de Rome*
by André Frénaud © Éditions Gallimard 1973.
English translation © Keith Bosley 1996.
Introduction © Peter Broome 1996.

ISBN: 1 85224 318 X

This edition published 1996 by
Bloodaxe Books Ltd,
P.O. Box 1SN,
Newcastle upon Tyne NE99 1SN.

Bloodaxe Books Ltd acknowledges
the financial assistance of Northern Arts.

Bloodaxe Books Ltd, the translators and the series editors
wish to thank the Ministère des Affaires Étrangères, Paris,
and the Service Culturel, the French Embassy, London,
for their assistance and for help given towards translation costs.

Cover printing by J. Thomson Colour Printers Ltd, Glasgow.

Printed in Great Britain by
Cromwell Press Ltd, Broughton Gifford, Melksham, Wiltshire.

CONTENTS

La Sorcière de Rome

Ce poème se compose de quinze mouvements:

Rome the Sorceress

This poem in fifteen movements:

GENERAL EDITORS' PREFACE

The Bloodaxe Contemporary French Poets series aims to bring a broad range of post-war French poetry to as wide an English-speaking readership as possible, and it has specific features which are designed to further this aim.

First of all, each volume is devoted to a complete, unabridged work by a poet. This is designed to maintain the coherence of what a poet is trying to achieve in publishing a book of poems. We hope that in this way, the particular sense of a poet working within language will be highlighted. Secondly, each work appears in parallel translation. Finally, each work is prefaced by a substantial essay which gives a critical appreciation of the book of poetry, of its place in its author's work, as well as an account of its social and intellectual context.

In each case, this essay is written by an established critic with a love of French poetry. It aims not only to be informative, but also to respond in a lively and distinctive way to the pleasures and challenges of reading each poet. Similarly, the translators, often poets in their own right, adopt a range of different approaches, and in every case they seek out an English that gives voice to the uniqueness of the French poems. The quality of the translations in the series has been widely recognised: two out of the first seven titles are Poetry Book Society Recommended Translations, an award given to only four books a year translated from any language.

Each translation in the series is not just faithful to the original, but aims to recreate the poet's voice or its nearest equivalent in another language: each is a translation from French poetry into English poetry. Each essay seeks to make its own statement about how and why we read poetry and think poetry. The work of each poet dovetails with others in the series to produce a living illustration of the importance of poetry in contemporary French culture.

TIMOTHY MATHEWS,
MICHAEL WORTON,
University College London

INTRODUCTION

The poetry of André Frénaud (1907-1993) is remarkable for its robust, dissatisfied questioning of the human condition: man in relation to life and death, his vain aspirations, his intrinsic contradictions, his never-ending skirmishes with glimmers of being and the energies of a tempting but impossible transcendence. His work moves in the unsettled space between self and the potent signs of otherness: signs which translate themselves simultaneously, however, as negation and eclipse, and leave the poet drawn on by renewed, by infinitely renewable, absence. Frénaud's poetry is not one of hope: it refuses the lures of faith, wishful consolations and the easy slippages of hypocritical thinking. Nor is it one of despair: content to give up the chase and enjoy life for the pleasures of its surfaces. It moves instead in what the author agrees to call 'le non-espoir' ('non-hope'): a state characterised by its taut philosophical integrity, not a neutral zone from which to evade commitment or further dilemmas of conscience, but a place of resistance and un-relieved quest. Frénaud belongs to the generation of Camus and Sartre, imbued by a sense of the 'absurd', of a life given for noth-ing, with no ascertainable transcendent value and unredeemed: the absurd which finds a mirror in the myth of Sisyphus, doomed to roll his rock to the verge of the summit only to see it fall, deprived of the solace of arrival but refusing to sit on his rock and succumb to what Camus calls the 'temptation of indifference'. A poem by Frénaud is alive with the energies of approach. Its problematical forms, pulled this way and that, racked by questions, bristling with divergent voices, carry not 'la musique de l'être' ('the music of being') but the broken harmonies, the dissonances, the disquieting hum, of a poetry caught betwixt and between: dragged, by its vocation, into the dynamo of universal contradiction, marked and moulded by the friction of opposites, and uselessly ejected, while awaiting the next encounter.

Under the floorboards

The characteristic title of a sombre collection of war-time poems by Frénaud is *Poèmes de dessous le plancher / Poems from under the floorboards*. The phrase emphasises the strength and complexity of his subterranean inspiration, of his underground movement, as it

9

were, drawn from the nether reaches, amidst the hidden conduits and constructional rubble. Born in the Burgundy mining town of Montceau-les-Mines, the author confesses the secret influence on him of that 'coal of childhood': images of descending and re-ascending to the daylight, of hewing in the darkness for a more precious matter, the premonition of a huge, unworked 'within' bulging with resources, the adoption of the image of layers of coal as a metaphor for the 'dark superimposed strata of the uncon-scious' (conceived more as a 'seething mass', however, than as something compacted and inert). A more recent text is ironically entitled *Mines de rien*, a colloquial phrase meaning 'all casual like', as if nothing were the matter, but which may also be taken literally as 'mines containing or revealing nothing'. For nothing could be less casual than Frénaud's persistent excavations, as the prose-poem *Position de défense / Defensive positions* indicates: 'Creuser, toujours creuser, la besogne est harassante à la longue!' ('Delving, always delving, the job wears you down in the end!'). And although his system of shafts, underground passages, cavities and impasses may not be said to yield nothing, the acquisitions are so dubious and elusive that he cannot be convinced that he has dug through finally to anything but the obscurities of himself. A strangely con-crete Narcissus: 'laboureur au labour de soi dans la nuit' ('plough-man ploughing himself in the night')'.

Frénaud's poems do not baulk at the closeness of the abyss. (He admits that it was Dostoyevsky rather than Freud who was, for him, the more potent revealer of the great dark gulfs in the human definition.) For where else would the advance-posts of poetry be found? Hence the innumerable varied bass-notes of his 'profonde voix'. 'Stir and rumble softly, my rumbler within,' and 'Grumble away, dull grumbler, song of my deep waters,' he writes respectively in *La profonde blessure / The deep wound* and its sister-poem *Dormir / To sleep*. Sometimes he speaks of his inner cellar, torn by the thunder flash and momentarily resplendent. Sometimes it is the 'âtre profond', a bottomless hearth burning inside, barely audible embers in a yawning alcove. More often his aspirations embrace the image of the tree, extravagantly, intricately rooted in the lower space, deep in the murmuring ground. 'A thousand roots,' he exclaims, almost with a note of awe, in his interviews with Bernard Pingaud, 'Yes, the poet sees himself as seeded earth. Or as if, comically, he found himself fertilised, just like a woman in labour!' Titles such as *Expansion de l'arbre / Tree expanding* or *Dans l'arbre ténébreux / In the tree's obscurity* compress the significance of the image, stressing Frénaud's visceral identification with all that is fed from below and its shadowy rising force groping for the light, finding forms, patterns and movements, while still anchored in the heaving density of a vast metamorphic organism. Many texts evoke an unmanageable force oozing from under the surface, from beneath the paving stones, through cracks and fissures in the rocks. It may be a sleeping warrior, the 'guerrier qui dort' who, according to Swedish legend, lies buried under the waters of the lakes of Värmland. It may be the ghost of the 1871 Commune and, by extension, the protest of the spirit of popular revolution, stirring anxiously beneath the cobbles of the Paris streets. Or 'le sang invisible/sous la craie blanche qui criait' ('the invisible blood/beneath the white chalk crying') speaking on behalf of the innocent martyrs of the Spanish Civil War. And, of all the disturbances or agents of subversion which – when 'la dentelle et les fleurs' ('lace and flora') gleam radiantly as a seemingly adequate antidote to the dilemmas of life and self – surge up and prompt the poet to say 'Pourtant j'entends gémir quelque part sous les peaux' ('And yet I hear a groaning under the skin somewhere'), none is more potent than the voice of the dead. Frénaud interrogates tombs. It is there – but equally well in any city street or lush or rugged countryside – that the underground stirs, aggressive, importunate, enigmatic, seeking its relationships anew. 'Je sens frémir l'appel de mes morts ignorés' ('I feel the quivering call of my unknown dead'), says the poetic voice in *L'Avenir ou l'Automne / Autumn or the Future*: vague belongings, compulsive but obscure heritages, restless inside the self. A key text, *Une bouffée des morts / A gust of the dead*, shows how the accumulated mass of the defunct can suddenly regain force and exert prerogatives, staking its claim physically, as it were, in the private passageways of speech, 'me touchant à la gorge' ('touching my throat'). It suggests how little it needs to dredge life from the 'années enfouies' ('the buried years'), and how many gaps and crevices, tiny Achilles' heels of time and perception, are there to provide access, unexpectedly. In the process, the poet breaks through the crust of his public identity – 'Je repars avec eux, loin dessous mon visage' ('I go journeying with them [the dead], deep beneath my face') – into an Underworld of collective memory, where he scarcely knows whether he is 'veilleur ou bien tombeau', watching over the dead and responsible for their continuing flame or else their deathly receptacle, their sarcophagus.

The problematics of the underground are condensed in the title of, and the following self-searching extract from, *Quoi dans la crypte? / What in the crypt?*:

À la suite de quelle randonnée nous étions-nous aventurés dans ce lieu obscur, pour nous confronter ou pour nous confondre, peut-être, avec une très ancienne présence...qui se dérobait au fur et à mesure que nous avancions, d'une excavation voûtée à d'étroites percées de lumière et d'un pilier à l'autre, remettant nos pas sur nos pas, et toujours vainement en proie...tellement que nous nous trouvâmes *interdits* – avant de revenir à nous, maigrement, puis de nous dissiper derechef dans la banalité industrieuse du jour.

By what strange trek had we ventured into this vague place, to be confronted or, perhaps, confused with an age-old presence...who slipped away as we moved further on, from a vaulted excavated site to narrow shafts of light and from one pillar to the next, replacing steps within our steps, and always vainly victims of...to such a length that soon we knew ourselves *prohibited* – before returning to our lean and hungry selves and fading back once more into the workaday banality of broad daylight.

The answer to the title-question snakes off in many different directions. The crypt is a nest of obscure forces. It may be the place of dream, the place where (as for the visionary Rimbaud who claimed, 'It is wrong to say "I think", one should really say, "I am thought"') one is incessantly 'dreamed upon'. 'Le rêve ne sait pas rêver assez profond' ('Dream cannot dream deep enough'), says Frénaud of this abyss of the imagination. But, at a lower level, the crypt is closer to the beasts: to primitive, panting energies seeking to extricate, reform, transcend themselves. In a text entitled *Trente ans après, Paris / Thirty years on, Paris*, which is a journey into time and space, into the twin labyrinth of memory and of a city's changing geography, the errant voice asks if it would succumb to fear were it to hear, 'épars sous le tombeau de pierres,/s'enfler le souffle du taureau éclatant?' ('dispersed beneath the tomb of stones,/the swollen breathing of the blaring bull?'). Other pieces are composed, and not least those war-time poems which bring embryonic 'nests of figures' squirming frighteningly to the surface, 'à l'orée des bêtes sombres' ('at the edge of the bestial dark'). This is the fringe where animal instincts and ambiguous allegiances move in the subconscious, roaming in the shadows to form the enemy within, the unacceptable self within the self: a world of phantasms, monsters, collapsing images from the dark.

Despite intimations of order, it is a world which drags one, through one's improvised defences and protective pretensions, into the unruly ferment of the universe in motion: the blind genetic magma, creating, destroying and recreating beyond measure. In the Pingaud interviews, Frénaud proposes this vision:

> Le chaos, la violence qui vient du profond, le monde de Dionysos ne se laissera jamais réduire à un cosmos défendable, et l'effort de l'homme pour se structurer en une conscience comme pour se représenter le monde par un système de pensée sera toujours à commencer. L'explosion des désirs jusqu'à l'écartèlement, l'énergie fécondante qui la soustend, l'éternelle origine avec l'éternelle remise en question. La poésie aussi surgit de là...

> The chaos, the violence which comes from the depths, the world of Dionysus will never let itself be reduced to a defensible universe, and man's attempt to structure himself into a consciousness, like his attempt to envisage the world according to a system of thought, must always be begun over and over again. The explosion of desires tearing one this way and that, the great inseminating energy which underlies it, the eternal source with its eternal calling into question. That, too, is the well from which poetry springs...

Whatever name one might give to all that moves beneath, and its obscure upthrust, this is a poetry which thrives on its intrinsic impossibility, on its stubborn negation of words, formulation and intellectual capture. Frénaud speaks of the 'Non médiateur' (the 'mediatory No'), that which elicits but refuses access, and of 'la profondeur du Profond' ('the depth of the Deep'), from which nothing is lacking, as 'la nourricière noire' ('the nourishing mother of dark'). (Could this also be a brooding synonym for the Sorceress who roams the underside of Rome?) Put simply, this is a poetry for which there is no light without dark, no face without the formless entrails of within, no edifice without the crumbling chasm, no life without the inner contradictions of its death. The abyss, which is its enemy, is also its breeding-ground. Such an ambivalent mediation as the source of poetry, and the complex circuitry of the subterranean voice, are nowhere better illustrated than in one of the fragments of *Fantasmes à Sienne / Imaginings in Siena*:

> La Sibylle vivait avec le mort dans une excavation ménagée plus bas. Il empruntait la voix de la femme pour laisser entendre une vérité au-delà des premiers signes. Le sens qui traversait, incertain, les paroles grommelées par cette fameuse devineresse, oscillait dans le cœur de ceux qui l'interrogeaient, à l'entrée de la caverne.

> The Sibyl lived with the dead one in an excavation hewn out even lower still. He assumed the woman's voice to transmit a truth extending far beyond the initial signs. The unsure meaning which traversed the muttered speech of that celebrated prophetess, wavered to and fro in the hearts of those who came to question her, at the cavern's mouth.

13

Cities

Frénaud is one of the great explorers of cities, and one of their most fertile myth-makers. Paris, Prague, Naples, Venice, Genoa and, on a more epic scale, Rome are among his privileged 'lieux d'approche' ('places of approach'). For they are all, or rapidly become so, places of quest and imaginative provocation. A piece entitled *Cette nuit-là, à Florence / That night, in Florence* makes the following bold distinction: 'Toujours les grandes villes m'ont troublé plus que la nature qui est trop claire, routes et rides étoilées, mamelons découverts, perspectives, nuages...' ('Always I have found big cities more disturbing than nature which is too patent, with its star-lit roads and wrinkles, bared hillocks, panoramas, clouds...') – adding that a village, for instance, rarely ever gives, and certainly not in any deep or searching sense, 'le sentiment de ce qu'on *n'atteint pas*' ('the sense of the *unattainable*'). And the passage continues, on the theme of 'la ville':

> Mais celle où l'on chemine pour la première fois, dont on ignore les dégagements et les encoignures, toujours elle apparaît étrangère, tout y besogne dans l'équivoque et inquiète le voyageur. Le rapprochement, pour chaque ville unique, de plusieurs styles que le temps a combinés [...] crépite soudain à la façon d'une métaphore.

> But the city that one walks through for the first time, unfamiliar with its routes of open access and its tight corners, invariably gives the appearance of foreignness, everything conspires towards ambiguity, disconcertingly for the traveller. With each individual city in turn, the bringing together of several styles interlocked through time crackles like a metaphor.

The city, then, for Frénaud, is a place of alienation, its unprecedented field of force prising one from the signposts of the self and proposing other combinations, other pathways, other poetic apparitions. It is as if he were walking in a vast dream, real and unreal, elaborated through time before one's very eyes, with palaces and porticos and modest houses jostling for precedence, amidst doorways and stairways, facades and fragments, openings and closures: a dream in which he loses something of himself and finds something of himself, flashes of recognition 'au miroir de l'étranger' ('in the mirror of foreign parts'), among the profusion of unknown forms and their confused patterns. A dubious exchange, as if somehow his quest and the city's quest – building its own identity in time, with the same processes of construction and destruction, shifts of centre, precariously conquered high ground and sprawling *bas lieux*, labyrinthine wanderings, overlaps and migrations – were one and the same.

The inexhaustible 'épaisseur' or inner density of the city draws Frénaud back again and again. It is there, perhaps more emphatically than with Mother-nature, that the vision of a womb looms large: the city as a great genetic receptacle, a crucible where human life is compounded, annulled and re-asserted ad infinitum. From under the monuments, from between the fractures of 'la pierraille frieuse' ('the crumbling of loose stones') – a more patent symbolic presence in Rome than in most other cities – a repressed energy permeates: a creative flux spawning and spurning alternately, crystallising and returning downwards into the impenetrable flood of history. A journey back to Paris after a significant break in time evokes the image of the heart as 'fidèle éponge' (a 'faithful sponge'), swelling like a piece of bread soaking and fermenting in the gutters of the city's streets in the stream of blurred perceptions and half-recognitions. It is in this sense that he refers to Paris as 'ma réserve songeuse' ('my reservoir of dream'): one city among the many where one ventures beyond the rational into a labyrinth of strange collocations and metaphoric partnerships, crossing the threshold into an underside closer to the obscurity of origins and, therefore, to the nocturnal languages of myth and dream. There are few poetries more receptive to 'les colloques du songe' ('the colloquia of dream'), for which the squares and passageways of the city are the great debating-chamber, ringing or whispering with echoes. It is as if one's merest step there were to disturb the shallow sleep of ages, and, with it, the enigma of the human definition, seen through the sprawling passages of one's latent fears, smudges of guilt and unconfessed desires.

Frénaud's city-poems are almost invariably mottled by the play of dark and light. Like the famous *Zone* of Apollinaire, a text which has come to symbolise the crisis of time, faith and identity at the heart of twentieth-century experience, they go through phases of day and night; they oscillate between moments of illumination and obscurity, between the diurnal and nocturnal. They lurch through a kaleidoscope of imaginary and real lights, through the unreliable colourings of memory, from the thin wine of normality to the lurid hues of apocalypse. Poetry passes between the sunny surfaces, the *divertimento* of scuffling streets, market-place activities, ornamental facades, the architectures of distraction, the daily froth; and the intimations of the underside and its shadowy significance, the dark discourse of the *vie profonde*. A brief text entitled *Les peurs de la nuit* / *Night-time fears* sketches, in a countryside context, what will be writ large and tortuously explored in

Rome: the dichotomy of the light and dark sides of experience, the recto and verso, the brocades of the outside and the murky, shifting lining. On the one hand, there is the light which lays to rest, comes to appease, re-lacquers things in place, which dissipates bad dreams as if they had no reality. On the other, when twilight takes hold, the cacophonous sounds, the frantic breathing, the fears, the nocturnal pursuits, the 'appartenances troublées' (the 'cloudy allegiances'), the switching of roles between hunter and hunted. As Frénaud writes in another piece devoted to the counterpoint of light: 'Sous le gazon ornementé, l'âme hagarde' ('Beneath the ornamental lawns, the haggard soul').

The city is the natural context for the unfurling of the theme of *errance*. *Où est mon pays? / Where is my homeland?* is the title of a key poem by Frénaud (words which have been transcribed on to the author's simple tombstone in the churchyard of Bussy-le-Grand in his native Burgundy). In *Les rues de Naples / The streets of Naples*, in the bewildering patterns of movement of the crowds, among provocative juxtapositions of ancient and modern, alongside images and ex-votos which may be signs or empty offerings, doorways or blocked alcoves, the wanderer tracks the vague orientations of an energy burning through the filaments of the urban scene. The eponymous hero of *Le Turc à Venise / The Turk in Venice*, a visitor of another faith, alights in Venice on a feast-day, a privileged interlude when there is 'a spirit abroad', as it were, and a secret communication seemingly to be fathomed. And in that maze, amidst the exits and entrances of waterways, he seeks an elusive centre and the meaning of his newly disoriented self: a strange pilgrim or alter ego who may or may not have been there, we are told, a thin, undocumented presence-absence (like the poet of *La Sorcière de Rome* who has engaged and disengaged, a 'fictional' traveller who has lived Rome, probed its depths, taken on its signs, given himself to its transformations and vanished like a ghost, yet another unverifiable voice or murmur in its drains). Similarly, in the taunting *silence* of Genoa (*Le Silence de Genova*), another street-walker moves like a somnambulist, as if magnetised by the challenge of the opening lines: *'Sauras-tu pressentir encore le rêve inscrit / ressassé dans ces pierres?'* (*'And will you sense once more the oft-repeated dream scored in these stones?'*). An exploration among the steps, towers, arches and side-tracks becomes a problematic itinerary among vestiges (and possible futures) of himself. A gathering force suggests some advent, some revelation, which insists on his commitment: in what way is his presence needed to accomplish it, and what is *it*? 'Une violente parole différée' ('a violent withheld word') is audible at the threshold, admitted and excluded, accepted and resisted at the same time: the power of the ever-imminent approaching as it recedes. He is its 'adversaire complice', its inimical accomplice: his 'interminable pas' (his 'never-ending tread') tracing enigmatic patterns but giving no access. Through all these cities – and Italy, for Frénaud, is a privileged ground bristling with buried life – he follows his *chemin des devins* (*diviners' route*) which is virtually synonymous with the *chemins du vain espoir* (*paths of impossible hope*). It is for this reason that one of the concluding lines of the cited poem reads, 'Où est mon pays? C'est autour du chemin' ('Where is my homeland? It's to right, left and centre of the route'): always peripheral, provisional, charted in approximations and inconclusive approaches.

Rome has a special place as a theatre of enquiry. For the poet whose first published poem was, paradoxically, *Epitaphe*, it is a place of epitaphs. The confrontation initiated in the perplexed overtures of a text such as *Des tombes vides au Père-Lachaise / The empty tombs of Père-Lachaise* acquires a greater historical and mythical depth in the Eternal City, this cemetery of the gods. What do all these death-defying structures mean? What original life-source do they still convey? What messages, if any, pass between the living and the dead? What paths of mediation are available to language? What meagre transcendence, what heritage, in their commentaries and commemorations, extracts and epigraphs, can words guarantee? Rome is not only a place where one feels legends moving under one's feet, stretching further and further away, layer after layer, in a kind of historical (and ultimately a-historical) *mise en abyme*: origins beyond origins. It is also, ambiguously, *berceau* and *tombeau* (*cradle* and *grave*): the birth-place of a civilisation and the cradle of a faith, and yet a place of ruins given to the stiffness of stones. It is a concentration of massive momentum and a spent force, a gravitational centre and a fragmented shadow, a place of pinnacles and the proof of decline and fall. As such, it dramatises the dilemma of beginnings and ends, of birth and death, which runs through Frénaud's work and clenches it with questions: 'Comme si le mot terminal n'était pas dans la gorge/à la naissance' ('As if the final word were not always in our throats/from birth') or 'Ta naissance t'étranglera-t-elle à la fin?' ('Will your birth in the end be the force that strangles you?'). So, in this extensive hearth where death burns, where the innumerable monuments offer their palliative, their antidote, their literal stop-gap to death while proving its dogged vitality, the poet asks if all is not a 'secret vide' (an 'empty mystery'), and whether these proud funeral stones are not 'des stèles pour nul événement?' ('monoliths commemorating no event').

In his 1968 collection *La Sainte Face / The Holy Face*, Frénaud has a section of texts entitled *Signes pour une fin du monde / Signs for an end of the world*. His exploration of Rome is, in some ways, a venture among such signs. He is writing, in the late twentieth century, amidst the collapse of laws and gods. Rome could, in a sense, take on the title of one of the author's most searching and personalised poems, *Tombeau de mon père / Tomb of my father*. It is the trigger for an encounter with a crumbling order, an authority now dismantled, and an enquiry into where the insuppressible energy of that order is due to transmigrate, and in what form. *Où est le père (Where is the father?)* is the question posed, and tortuously elaborated, in another more recent poem; while in the Pingaud interviews Frénaud acknowledges the existence, deep within himself, of a persistent need to justify himself before the 'tribunal of the father', even in negation and revolt, and despite poetic images widely invoked among his texts of 'la révocation du père tout-puissant' ('the dismissal of the omnipotent father').

La Sorcière de Rome is therefore written in a problematic vacancy, amidst 'les ruines de Dieu' and the confusion which ensues. It slips into the vertigo of the missing God and broaches the abyss of impossible resurrection. It is a challenge to the established myths of order, to voices on high which pretend to legislate. It is a dark investigation of the bases of faith. So, in a city where the external trappings of religion are eminently prominent, where facile synonyms of salvation abound, the poet delves into a dubious history of blood, violence and innocent martyrdom, of sacrifices expiating nothing, of false apostles and perversions of the word. It is the black blood of the Cross which spills loose, still seeking some redemption, and not its gilded triumph. Which Lord and Master does one see there, in that faith which fragments into a thousand faces, if not all the usurpers of his absence: tyrants, executioners and deceptive intercessors? As if in a waxworks gallery or a disturbing hall of mirrors, one makes out the dehumanised features of the Grand Inquisitor and reads the sinister dialectic of order and oppression, Master and slave (accompanied by threats of mutilation and castration). One sees the travesties of the will to power, the self-mystifications and aberrations of the history of spirituality: how the breath of Revolution, political or religious,

18

whether in the Moscow trials of 1935 or in the establishment of the Church through the ages can curdle into an orthodoxy, a self-protective hierarchy, with watchwords, doctrinal pronouncements, a specious triumphalism (backed, at worst, by false confessions, rigged evidence and lies).

If Rome enables Frénaud, as he does in his famous modernistic version of *Les Rois Mages / The Magi*, to explore the tragic dilemmas and dimensions of le '*non-espoir*', stressing the modulations of loss and frustration rather than the promise of arrival and eschewing all 'illusions consolatrices', it is not that it is a place of death and negation. On the contrary, the energy of its contradictions – its rise and fall, its tensions of ancient and modern, its testimonies of fragility and resurgent strength, its doses of sacred and profane, its faith and faithlessness, its rare equation of being and nothing-ness – make it a privileged arena in which to register the workings of that *coincidentia oppositorum*, the oscillations and turbulences of which are the nearest equivalent that one will know of the unre-solved totality of Being. It is therefore a place of confluences, where the receptive self of poetry is caught between streams, alternately annihilated and re-established, drawn into the flood and restored to shorelines. So, if Rome embodies the collapse of great promises, it is for that very reason, the cavern where one can chase their echoes and revive, if only problematically, their rumbling field of force. And if her history tells the story, as force-fully and enigmatically as that of any city, of visitations born to die, then poetry comes to interrogate what has been built, if only as a futile or precarious gesture, on that powerful eclipse. Rome, then, is a massive 'ouverture ontologique' or ontological opening. It is the ambivalent illustration, pulled between Christian and pagan, God and gods, and demi-divinities of all shades and com-plexions, of 'la trace de l'homme en proie du divin' ('the trace of man tormented by the divine'): man with his 'sempiternelles fables' (his 'everlasting fables') and harbouring his 'vieilles illusions média-trices' (his 'age-old dreams of intercession'). Rome calls one to interrogate, not only 'signs for the end of a world', but signs for the beginning of a world, which are perhaps interchangeable or one and the same. For Frénaud speaks, not simply of the hollow left by the death of gods, but of 'l'Absence antérieure et postérieure aux dieux': the absolute Absence which pre-dates and post-dates all gods, and into which men pour their sacred representations, their des-perate desires, their ingenious will for order and consolation. The Absence that recreates itself, indefatigably, and belies monuments.

Rome has another important value for Frénaud. Not only does its intricate geography merge to become a suggestive labyrinth of the mind, with its chiaroscuro of hope and aridity, possession and loss, direction and disorientation; but it offers itself as a searching metaphor for the functions of poetry, so that the exploration of one is simultaneously, consubstantially, an exploration of the other. Numerous texts by Frénaud, notably *Le Château et la quête du poème / The Castle and the quest of the poem*, pose the problem of the construction of a poem and, more widely, of a whole book of poems (with its various questions of juxtaposition, overlapping, overlaying, concerns of coincidence and contrast, continuity and disruption, alliance and irony, reinforcement and renouncement, unity and diversity). The poem, in its structural hesitations, lingering alternatives, writings and re-writings, is 'l'innombrable édifice', the incalculable or innumerable edifice. Its architecture, in closing, must open; in imprisoning and crystallising flux, must reinvigorate and release it; in verbalising the unlimited, must guarantee its virtuality. A walk in Rome, through its monuments, amidst its compacted memoirs, is an encounter with one's own multi-layered memories, creative aspirations and yearnings for transcendence. It is a tight-rope walk between construction and ruin, the 'château' and the 'abîme'. The city's own embattled composition, in time and space, is in the image of that of the text: an ambivalent structure, raised and dashed, fashioned and ravaged, replete and empty. Pointing out Frénaud's tendency to exalt and belittle poetry simultaneously, to endow it with the most grandiose or extravagant ambitions while shrinking it with contempt and a sceptical irony, Pingaud says: 'Il n'est guère de textes de vous concernant l'expérience poétique où la poésie ne soit à la fois magnifiée et dépréciée' ('There is scarcely a text by you on the subject of poetic experience in which poetry is not simultaneously glorified and disparaged'). Rome, in its triumph and decline, its massive architecture and ruined fragments, its heights and depths, is the perfect setting for such an illustration. There is one further crucial link between the city, the so-called Eternal City, and the anguished enquiries of poetry. In *Haeres*, a title which means (among other things), *inheritor*, Frénaud not only shows himself caught in a struggle with his own parentage (which is both an indebtedness and a lack, acceptance and refusal, a tenderness and a resentment), but probes the enigma of poetry as heritage: Is the poem merely an illusion of prolonged duration? What kind of legacy, if any, does it ensure? Does it re-admit one, as a rigid monument of words, into the problematic ebb and flow of the poetic experience and its momentary confluence of forces? Is it, indeed, a transmissible value? What effective mediation does it create and is it, in the end, only a legacy from self to self, the poet inheriting his own estate, obscurely acquiring echoes of who he was: a homeland and a place of exile?

Time and Motion

If, in a poem entitled *Pays perdu / Lost land*, Frénaud can return on a pilgrimage to his native region only to conclude, 'Ici, il n'y a plus d'autrefois' ('Here, there are no more yesterdays'), then that is certainly not the case with Rome. Like the Baudelaire of 'J'ai plus de souvenirs que si j'avais mille ans' ('I have more memories than if I were a thousand years'), the poet of *Ancienne mémoire* writes: 'Déjà, le front contre la pierre,/de mille années je me souviens' ('And even now, my forehead pressed against the stones,/I recollect a thousand years'). He is a writer for whom no time is expended, no time inert. *Vieux pays* speaks of 'ceux qui ont gardé l'oreille de leur enfance' ('those who remain in the confidence of their childhood'), hearing the voices of one's own deepest roots, the message of things awakening from some age-old sleep: breaths from afar, 'le langage de l'autrefois dans l'âme bouleversée' ('words of yesteryear in the disrupted soul'). It is the continued vitality of the past, not as a place of relics but as a power for change, whose latent momentum alone ensures the future: 'Pas encore finie ma vie puisque j'avoue/l'autrefois...' ('Not yet at an end my life since I admit to/yesteryear'), says Frénaud, savouring this reversal of perspectives. So, the city is an ancient palimpsest, written over innumerable times: through its streets, in a complex space-time equation, the searcher reads in discontinuous snatches 'les archives des journées disparues' ('the archives of lost days').

The dark enigma of birth obsesses Frénaud's work: its promise and its purposes, its blind alleys and lost directions, its formations and malformations. Hence the prominence of the image of the egg: is it broken once and for all? what emerges from it? how long must creation run its time? is there a return to origins? what signs can be gleaned of the proof of rebirth? What the poet never doubts is that 'Je nais toujours' ('I am still in the process of birth'). This means not only an extraordinary awareness of the underground fermentation still in force, but a sensitivity to all inaugural movements, the scattered minor ripples and reverberations of the one great inaugural movement transfusing all. Its muffled voice, 'la rumeur dont nous cherchions l'origine depuis le départ' ('the murmur whose source we had been seeking from the very start'), waxes and wanes, is more or less insistent, more or less audible, coaxing and communicating, teasing and tormenting. The question of origins looms large. Where, and by what detours, has one lost the thread of childhood? How does one re-connect with the very depths, the furthest flung outposts, the most tenuous continuities, of the self? Metaphors of innocence, surfacing through the thick fabric of a world out of sorts, seemingly at odds with itself from time immemorial, are frequently invoked. As are, more generally, pictures of innocent suffering, which nothing justifies and to which nothing brings remission. All of which raise the suspicion, voiced in *Haeres*, of a fatally flawed creation: 'Le berceau se trouvait-il au départ un peu fêlé?' ('Was the cradle, from the outset, somewhat cracked?').

It is a poetry structured (and disrupted) by cycles, drawn into the wheel of successive seasons, births and deaths, destructions and resurrections. It contemplates, with a kind of awed perplexity, that tireless self-contradictory momentum into which human history has been inscribed: what Frénaud calls the 'éternel éphémère renouveau' (the 'eternal ephemeral renewal'), time proceeding with a manic, panic (Pan-like) inevitability. 'Tout s'engouffre dans la roue pour activer ce qui viendra' ('All is plunged into the wheel to speed what is to come'), he writes and, with a sharper paradox, 'tout s'échappe et fait trace' ('All vanishes and leaves its mark'). The story of Rome is its living illustration. Actions which purport to have changed the world now stand idle, as their own monumental travesties. Sacrifices, martyrdoms and massacres have foundered in the anonymous eddies of history.

Frénaud calls time a 'faux monnayeur': the counterfeiter, playing false, dealing in false coinage. It turns the authentic interchange into a lost encounter, the valid into the invalid, the promised into the unacceptable. Hence the upsurge of the figure of Janus with his 'double profil' (one of the many Roman gods uncovered in *La Sorcière*): opening and closing doors, switching rectos with versos, donning and removing masks. The great flux of being is simultaneously *saisie* and *dessaisie*, possession and dispossession, fleeting capture and relinquishment. It is felt as tremors *entre centre et absence*: the vital force traversing one but of which one is only the periphery, movements which are a fire in the dark and then a blanched disaster. A simple two-verb paragraph, poised at a strategic position in *Incertitude de l'aube / Uncertain dawn* reads: 'Anticipaient... Se dissipaient' ('Anticipate...Evaporate'). The passage from one to the next is virtually instantaneous. One slips from near future to already irretrievable past through the hollow or erosion, that unretentive space, which is the present. It is not surprising that Frénaud should write, 'l'*Être*, pour nous qui nous trouvons là,/c'est une autre façon pour nommer le *Rien*' ('Being, for us who are abandoned here, is but another name for Nothingness'). Nor that a poem concerned with taunting glimpses at the limit of the perceptible, entitled *Reproches à l'être caché / Reproaches addressed to the hidden being*, should invoke that 'Visiteur pervers, qui n'interviens que pour me tenir plus fermement éloigné de toi, entretenu dans mes contradictions geignardes...' (that 'Visitor perverse who intervenes with one sole aim in view: to keep me even further far away, held in my state of contradiction and complaint') – a being dedicated to the infinite forms of absence and prolonged pursuit.

Frénaud clings to the crevices of time, lingers by its doorways. Feast-days and celebrations are the potential passageways of time: the Achilles' heel, perhaps, the vulnerable joint where one can gain purchase and seek re-entry. In commemorating the past, they suggest a transferred heritage and a renewal. They give access to gusts of the original energy which shaped events, wrought transformations, seemingly re-directed the course of history. They promise new advents, presage epiphanies. That such commemorations are a problematic concern in Frénaud's work is clear from such titles as *Noel interdit / Forbidden Christmas* and *Pauvre fête / Meagre festival,* or a question like 'Pourquoi la fête?' ('Why the celebration?'), which seals the structure of a whole text devoted to the possibilities of faith. Rather than proving perennity or that time can stay true to itself beyond change and erasure and retain its promise undiminished, such feast-days (and the Roman calendar abounds with them) re-emphasise, for the author of *La Sorcière*, the inevitability of doings and undoings, all the short leases that one holds, all the cracks in one's pretentions to seize eternity. They are a focal point for the ambivalences of time: refreshing the dead, giving momentary access to an 'ancienne mémoire', tying past with present in such a way that one might almost believe in a continuity of purpose and see all sacrifices as justified; but then closing doors to aggravate loss, alienation, clashes of age and youth, and the difficulty of accepting the remorseless perpetuation of a world from which we shall be obliterated. 'Plénitude venue des vieux temps...O ravagée!' ('Plenitude sprung from ancient times...O ravaged unity!'), writes Frénaud. Rome will be the theatre of this oxymoron: a city undone in the fullness of time.

Fires of the Sorceress

Rome is a place of gods and goddesses, father-figures and latent mothers. *La Sorcière* illuminates their contest, their repressed tensions, the ambiguities of their alternative values and respective sways. Frénaud has revealed that, after the writing of and in contrast to *Tombeau de mon père*, the new fifteen-movement epic poem could be seen as 'un "tombeau de la mère" qui n'ose pas dire son nom' ('a "tomb of the mother" that dare not speak its name'): that is, a disguised, elusive, metaphorical commemoration which delves into a magma of confused, conflicting emotions and dubious allegiances. A communication, not so much with the mother of flesh and bood nor with specific memories or tokens of a human relationship, but with the age-old female force which she embodies, the tantalising, frightening, destabilising feminine pole which, in attracting, negates and invalidates. In celebrating this presence (this presence-absence, in that it is always lost and found, written deep within yet inaccessible), the poet is, in a sense, idolising and burning his own witch, whom he loves and fears, fears to love and loves to fear – a vast ritual ceremony enacted, ironically yet necessarily, in the city of the Holy Father. Frénaud's work persistently confronts and casts into doubt the veracity of the Father. In *L'Étape dans la clairière / The halt in the clearing*, another extensive poem dedicated, significantly, to *Aeternae memoriae matris*, one reads: 'Il n'est pas de père. Il n'est de retour en un sein vivant' ('There is no father. There is no return to a living breast'). While one of his Wise Men in *Les Rois Mages* pauses at another crossroads of the journey to ask if the quest is an approach to truth or a subconscious evasion, an act of courageous self-exposure or a cowardly self-protection under the shifting, not to say shifty, star of a self-invented god: 'Est-ce un dieu qui m'attire,/père cruel ou le fils de mon cœur lâche?' ('Is it a god who draws me on, callous father or the son of my craven heart?'). In chasing the call of the Sorceress, the new poetic pilgrim is returning to a more authentic source, a more tangible and intangible divinity: by no means more reassuring however, but one with its deeper enigmas, more disturbing conflicts and pungent perplexities. A faceless figure closer to, tantamount to, 'la cavité d'origine', and therefore beyond the clasp of love or words. Critics have stressed the great looming presence – and the fast-receding elusiveness – of 'la Femme absolue' ('Woman absolute') in Frénaud's poetry: Woman absolute who defies the imagination, generates myths and metaphors, draws emotions over the edge, forces one radically to reconsider the role and status of the self. An insatiable, inexhaustible genetic force, she can assume all forms, adopt and reject in turn the dressings and dramatisations of all passing imagery: the sloughed skins of would-be conquests and half-fathomed relationships. She is seen at times as the woman warrior, the huntress, Amazon or 'guerrière'. Poems such as *La chasse / The chase* or *Jeune Amazone et son ombre / Young Amazon and her shadow* evoke the burning for capture, the boundless quest for prey of which one becomes oneself the prey, embodied in such female figures, inciters of obscure desire, who flash momentarily into vision from the thicket, tracing trajectories burned out before one can follow. The theme acquires one of its most complex treatments in *La mort d'Actéon / The death of Acteon*, where one spell-binding glimpse of the goddess Diana, scattered in water, becomes a swirling well of contradictions: desire and prohibition, sensuality and abstraction, temptation and refusal, conquest and surrender. The eponymous hero/hunter becomes himself the quarry, shredded and devoured by his own dogs turned against him, plunged into the mysterious 'parloir souterrain' (the 'underground parlour', synonymous with the void and vertigo of the poetic word tugged beyond reason): at first a cleft in the universe, then an abyss of 'paroles noires' ('dark words') and verbal delirium, opened up, not simply by the paradoxes of Diana, the goddess fulfilling her function by reverting from hunted to huntress, but through her, by the 'Grande Mère à profusion', the universal Mother proliferating through all time and space, who reintroduces one into the *innommable*, that which has no name, the unspeakable, and engulfs one. Or it may be the Sibyl flirting with death and divination at the cavern's mouth. Or the Gorgon of *Parole de la Gorgone au Serpent / The Gorgon's word to the Serpent*, also playing ominously at the entrance to her cave, tantalising, postponing; opening her legs or the two great rivers (of self and other drawing one fatefully between) to reveal that 'ventre abîme et feu qui rougeoie,/originel, terminal, ennemi' ('womb abyss and glowing fire,/first and last, inimical').

The manifestations of the 'Grande Mère' in Frénaud's poetry are innumerable. In a poem entitled *Les Mères*, he writes (and it is

noticeable that *La Sorcière* begins also with the words 'La vieille...'
and ends with the 'très antique sibylle', as if imprisoned within
that vast embrace): 'Même au tombeau, la vieille ne nous tiendra
pas quitte,/elle a sur nous mainmise, nous tenant dans la poix'
('The age-old Woman, even in the grave, will never clear us of
our debts,/she threatens us with seizure, keeps us in pitch black').
Though frequently identified with the great Earth-Mother, the
original womb conceiving and replenishing, and with the irresistible
maternal maturity taking all things from seed to ampleness, she is
an ambivalent, untrustworthy *médiatrice*. As the oldest of our
fiancées, she is the reservoir of birth and death. She is also the
well of the inexplicable, perhaps even of the absurd: of life which
will not divulge its meaning, of creation bound for its own expen-
diture and annulment, of things summoned only to be dismissed.
She is therefore not a comforting matron, but a ravaging unrea-
son. Hence the haunting presence, endlessly resurrected here, of
the so-called 'Mère folle' or 'Mad Mother':

> nous ne créons plus de dieux, nous sommes délaissés.
> La Mère folle est partout avec nous dans la danse
>
> we no longer create gods, we are abandoned to our fate.
> The Mad Mother is everywhere whirling with us in our dance
>
>   *
>
> Folle très, se tenait la Mère et cachée.
> Contre la loi, contre les usages. Dans l'usage aussi,
> immémoriale en de certains jours triomphant.
> Aujourd'hui la même là, partout, sans répit,
> la Mère folle.
>
> Mad in the extreme, there stood the Mother, hiding still.
> Versus the law, versus all common practices. And yet within those
>   practices,
> timeless yet surging in triumph on certain days.
> Today, as was and ever shall be, there, and everywhere, without respite,
> the great Maternal madness.

As the enormous and frightening antidote to order, the established,
the reliable status quo, congealed time and stability, she can veer
more towards nightmare than the dream of creation. She can release
disorientation and chaos in the squirming, avid genetic offshoots
which she breeds: 'marâtre à faire surgir mille serpents jaunes/des
œufs innocents renfermés' ('stepmother conjuring up a thousand
yellow snakes/from the innocent enclosure of the egg'). She bursts
from the corsetry of paternalistic regimes with a huge force for
change and a subversive energy. She is 'la femme au centre creux'

('hollow-centred woman'), not permanence and plenitude but a fomenting, aching chasm. She is the mother of the metamorphic and the unassimilable. For this reason, her 'folie' is to be preserved at all costs as a kind of salvation: a genetic inebriation, a fever of the unfinished, an excess of dissident force denying its own containment, an insidious prickle of renewal. Through her, in league with her, the poet knows himself as overspill ('Je me déborde, inachevé'). She is the *folie* of our discontent. The Mother, then, nestling in him and lurching beyond him, who embodies the fundamental non-acceptance: a hatred of the finitude of the self and its relapse towards compromise, contentment and self-satisfaction.

'Revolutionary Woman' makes her frequent forceful appearances in the compositional whole of Frénaud's work: an agent of disturbance in the architectural arrangements, gusts of rebellion, threat and exposure between the stones and structural beams (or, in the case of Rome, the ramparts, pillars and colonnades). The brief epigraph heralding the entrance of the *Énorme figure de la déesse Raison* on the stage of the poem of that title reads: 'N'aie pas peur des lamproies du profond sommeil, petit écolier de la Révolution' ('Be not afraid of the lampreys of deep sleep, little pupil of the Revolution'). And she, in the profuse and vibrant monologue which follows, describes herself as 'incendiaire sirène' ('inflammatory enchantress'): hardly a force of reason, in the accepted sense, but an aggressive *raison d'être*, deeply worked through the currents of creation, irrepressibly pursuing her births and disturbing the peace. She is the goddess who weakens and topples gods, pre-dates and supersedes them. But she, too (and Rome as a city of statues is her graveyard as well as her bed), has been celebrated and ceremonialised, petrified, officialised and shamed: a Genetrix of stone, robbed of herself. Hence her lament:

> Ils m'ont réduite à n'être qu'une statue de gloire,
> enfermée dans les carrés déserts de leurs places [...]
> Ils m'honorent apaisée par le nombre et la pierre,
> non plus beauté dans le malheur mais protectrice encore
> de leur serment qu'ils ignorent avoir perdu,
> moi, la tempête qui retroussais leurs dieux, ils m'adorent.

> They have reduced me to no more than a glorious statue,
> lost in the closed compartments of their public squares [...]
> They honour me appeased by symmetries and harmonies of stone,
> no longer raging beauty in misfortune but the patron still
> of their allegiances relinquished unbeknown,
> and now, the tempest who once whipped the edges of their gods, they
>   tamely worship me.

In Frénaud's last poetic collection, similar figures continue to loom to the fore. There is the *Petite Révolutionnaire / Girl of Revolution*, whose burning eyes taunt the sun as she wanders the roads with an 'absurd frenzy', exciting but accepting no lover, cleaving as she goes, fired by an incurable energy. There is also the poet's verbal double of Picasso's *La Femme qui pleure / The Crying Woman* of 1939: more a savaged victim than a presiding goddess, one might think, but one who, through blood and tears, and in her terrible fragmentation and deformity (including the eyes at odds with each other), can stand as the only fully adequate symbol and intercessor of a world in disarray, off its axis, loose at the joints, 'un monde que l'on ne pourrait désormais FIXER' ('a world henceforth beyond all point of anchorage'). Elsewhere, too, as in *Chuchotements aux Oliviers / Whispers on the Mount of Olives*, woman, though pitched in the dark of the mind and bearing wounds, emerges as the supreme truth, and the appropriate model and 'divinity' for humanity: woman like a great uprising, taking on the weight of what must tear her apart and leave her.

The *Sorcière* lurks in the margins of the same family. She is the heretical firebrand, the woman of no way, with no *droit de cité*, incompatible with establishment and order, banished from the centre, feared for what she might inflame and disrupt. She is outlawed, martyred and made scapegoat, but lives on in the underground of covert dreams and half-caressed allegiances. She is the force, possessed by devils, one might say, through whom possession is dispersed, scattered as a value. She prevents the thickening and skinning over of all status quos. One of the many rebel-figures in Frénaud's work, she is virtually synonymous with a yawning, burning Absence (the insatiable ontological *élan*). 'À la médiation du feu' ('To the mediation of fire'), proposes Frénaud, as the central formula of a poem of poetic 'toasts' or invocations to a guardian spirit. Her fire is that of the desire to know, the desire to be, always raging unfulfilled: or just of Desire on the loose, not knowing of what. There could be no more lucid analysis of the role of the Witch/Sorceress than the author's remarks in interview with Bernard Pingaud:

> Que l'ordre romain perdure à travers des formes successives – le monde antique, le christianisme des mosaïques saintes, mais aussi ce triomphalisme baroque, qui va dégénérer en sa caricature avec le palais de Vittorio Emmanuele – il ne saurait pour autant étouffer la voix de *la Sorcière*. Voix de l'innombrable protestation du désir insatisfait, de la part inacceptable, non rachetable, d'injustices et de cruautés, avec ce que pareille protestation implique d'espérance, d'espérances trahies et,

dirais-je, à un certain niveau d' 'innocence'. *La Sorcière*, sous de multiples figures, gronde tout au long du poème. Et c'est elle qui est victorieuse à la fin, voix de notre irréductible malheur.

Even if the order which is Rome lives on eternally through its successive forms – the ancient world, the Christianity of the holy mosaics, but also that baroque triumphalism which ultimately degenerates into its own caricature with the Victor Emmanuel palace – it is not, for that reason, powerful enough to stifle the voice of *the Sorceress*. The voice of the infinite protest of unsatisfied desire, the voice of the unacceptable, of injustice and cruelty in the world, with all that such a protest implies of hope, of hopes betrayed and, I would add, a degree of 'innocence'. *The Sorceress*, in her innumerable guises, reverberates through the poem from end to end. And it is she who finally emerges victorious, the voice of the insurmountable human tragedy.

She is, then, the ragged patroness of unredeemed pain, the mouthpiece of dried blood and sacrificed ignorance (innocence) which receive no truth in return, the shadowy protector of all those wayward possibles of the imagination which drive invisible wedges and open cracks in the totalitarian conspiracy. She is also a revolutionary darkness. Referring to Mozart's *The Magic Flute* in an essay on the painter and sculptor Raoul Ubac, Frénaud quotes the words: 'Qui triomphera, de la Reine de la Nuit ou des prêtres du soleil?' ('Who will emerge as victor, of the Queen of Night or the priests of sunlight?'). There is no doubt as to the answer in *La Sorcière*. Subsuming the potency of all other female deities glimpsed in dream and myth, she is the 'Reine de la Nuit'. In her vertigo, in her shreds of unity undone, in her fiery encroachments retreating instantly to the margins, she is the irreducible enemy of High Priests. 'Malheur à ceux qui savent,/aux grands prêtres sauvés,/ aux puissants satisfaits' ('Woe betide the knowers of truth,/the salvation of high priests,/the complacency of the mighty'), proclaims a voice in *Whispers on the Mount of Olives*. And if, through this rejection, the Father is dead or dying, murdered or negated by his own son, is she, then, the dubious mother of the self-searching Oedipus, now at large in a world of floating reins: the 'médiatrice de l'amour interdit' ('mediator of forbidden love')?

The descent into the labyrinth of Rome, with its crypts and buried yesteryears, is indeed a quest for love. It is a plunge into 'la nuit maternelle' ('the maternal dark'). It is a clutching at the breast of birth: not simply that symbolised in the city streets by the dugs of the she-wolf omnipresent in statues, metal plaques and everyday coinage, nor by that upturned image of the same formed by the heaving hills of Rome like some Earth-goddess suckling her eager multitude, but that which comes to obsess the dreams of the 'Roi Mage' in his star-haunted journey: 'Et la grande mamelle se gonfle, si noire et sans pourtour,/si violemment silencieuse' ('And the great breast swells, so black and boundary-less,/so violently silent'). Roma...Amor: Rome is love in the mirror, translated back, seen in reverse. It is an ever-available palindromic passageway to its own erotic depth. It is not surprising that one of Frénaud's most searching poems should be entitled *La Noce noire / Black wedding*. It is tormented by the question: 'Où va-t-elle apparaître, la fiancée,/dans les débarras de la nuit, à la faveur du supplice?' ('Where will she next appear, our betrothed,/in the junkyards of the night, by the grace of agonies?'). Those who seek her, dancing with her in their dreams, memories and mirages, are caught in a terrible game of hot and cold, pursuing an image or the semblance of an image which will not hold still, never settle on a single value. Similarly, in *Le navire négrier / The slave ship*, the ship deserted by its once-beloved captain (now irretrievable, perhaps dead) receives a mysterious female visitation, whose face one is never sure of having seen: an ambivalent presence who guides and confuses directions, brings promise and impossibility, instils hope and despair, sleeps with the crew and keeps her distance as perfect purity and the inaccessible figurehead.

The desire to bring together from the extremes of youth and age, and reconcile, the first fount of life and its distorted end- (but never-ending) product, innocence and fallen creation, generates a host of images in Frénaud's work, the most commanding of which is that of the Virgin, most typically (as titles such as *La Noce noire* and *Le navire négrier* would suggest) a black Virgin, uncomfortably close to the violence and perversions of the world, as if unable to dissociate herself from them. She who revitalises the movements of the slave ship and the rhythmic labours of *la Noce noire* bound for their shadowy union is timeless: 'Ils ne savaient pas depuis quand ils dansaient avec elle,/la vierge qu'ont noircie les boissons et les coups' ('They did not know how long their dance with her had been,/this virgin blackened by the drink and marks of violence'). She is immaterial and incarnate, respected and abused, venerated and defiled. Innocent but ravaged, immaculate but tarred in the depths of sexual experience, the image of the Virgin Mother haunts these various pathways, stands as their crossroads or possible meeting-point. Hence the appeal: 'Quelle vierge nous gardera/de tout ce qui souffle de l'ombre,/soufre et malodorants palus?' ('What virgin shall save us/from all that breathes hard from the shadows/sulphur and the stench of swamps?'). Hence this transcription of a small fresco seen in a chapel on a journey through the Ticino, a tense reminder of the blood of life and the blood of pain, the milk of kindness and the precious life-source gluttonously drained:

Couronnée d'épines, c'est elle qui l'est.
Et le lait qui sort
            de ses seins qui gonflent
– Ô flux de la femme, et don de la femme –
c'est le sang toujours
            qui nourrit le lait,
c'est le sang qui souffre...

Now it is she who is crowned with thorns.
And the milk which comes
            from her swelling breasts
– Oh womanly flow, and womanly gift –
is forever the blood
            which feeds the milk,
is the blood of suffering still...

Hence also this vision of the travesty of birth, warped into a nightmare of mutilation and distortion: 'Qu'ai-je aperçu entre tes grands genoux, vierge-mère,/sinon ce misérable coq en déplumé,/tordant son cul vers nous' ('Virgin mother, what have I seen between your massive knees,/but this wretched cockerel with its feathers shed,/ twisting its backside down at us'). The dream of harmonious creation, ideally rounded, fed from an untainted source, envisaged in the image of the egg or the perfect breast, is threaded through *La Sorcière*: creation with no hair-line cracks, no rifts, no pangs of torn flesh and irreconcilable conflict. Frénaud, speaking to Pingaud, has added his own searching commentary. In *La Sorcière de Rome*, the accent is more patently on the Virgin Mother than the child, he says. And, through that figure, one sees the tragic confrontation of 'le manque fondamental' ('fundamental lack') and 'une plénitude perdue ou imaginée' ('a lost or imagined plentitude'). She, as the daughter of our failures and the product of our hope, has justifiably emerged as the infinitely pliable Mother of humanity. She offers herself in sacrifice: intercessor and mediator for desperate imaginations. She is our helpmate and scapegoat. As Frénaud writes: 'Ce que la Vierge va compenser, c'est ce poids de mal et de malheur, tout ce qui donne à l'homme l'impression de l'échec de sa vie. Voilà ce dont elle s'est chargée, bouc émissaire *sublime*' ('What the Virgin comes to make good is the weight of evil and unhappiness, all that gives man the impression of the disaster of his life. That is what she has taken upon herself, as our *sublime* scapegoat').

The Sorceress may seem at a far remove from the Virgin-Mother, but in 'broaching the siren', as the author puts it, he is touching the unstable fringe of the same age-old woman: the same absence, the same marginality, the same unassimilability or outlawed potency which shrinks back into the wings, still working its spells, promising miracles but driving desires to distraction. Woman, indeed, as 'la fournaise d'absence' ('the furnace of absence'), obscurely showing love for what it is: a renewable destruction and reconstruction of the self, an ambition to transform otherness into sameness, a possible joy and an inescapable metaphysical failure.

Crossroads of the Voice

Frénaud's poetry is not univocal. Unity of voice evades it no less than unity of metaphysical capture and possession. Indeed, poetry survives only at that price – in the discovery that it is at variance with itself – and in the ability to make a virtue of necessity. It is knowing that he is condemned in this way that the poet says, 'Pourquoi je n'aime la voix que fêlée?' ('Why do I only love the voice that's cracked?'), and that, as compassionate observer of one of his self-searching female characters, he asks, 'en quelle eau basse/ déchirera-t-elle ses propres lèvres?' ('In what deep waters/will she tear apart her living lips?'). In taking the plunge, the poem discovers, at the risk of disintegration and vertigo, its own division or multiplicity of voice.

Frénaud has a text entitled *La double origine du langage / The double origin of language*. It shows the poet labouring to match his language to another elusive voice, a low murmur or mere rumour in the inner ear aroused as he speaks, sprung from a source of which he was once arguably a part: the sound of a lost connection which he seems vaguely to recognise and which he is called on to restore. He describes the tentative discourse torn from his mouth, arduously wrought, inadequately miming the slippery prestige of some 'syllabe initiatrice, dominatrice': an initiatory, overriding 'syllable' or primal utterance which, having moved and mobilised, withdraws as one progresses, as if intimidated by the very momentum that it has unleashed. Its staging of the multiple dilemma of language, creating texts which reflect deeply on their own nature and origins, makes Frénaud's work one of the most modern of its time. *Dans ma voix / In my voice* not only dramatises the 'otherness' of and in the voice, rehearsing whether it is immanent or transcendent, passing through or emanating from the self, but vigorously hovers in that 'Vent debout entre soi et soi' (that 'Wind rising high between self and self'), which interposes its airy but prohibitive rift, prompting the question, 'Où se place l'indécise, l'indélébile / fêlure?' ('Where does it draw its line, the indelible, indecisive / crack?').

In a note appended to his final collection of poems, Frénaud states that 'généralement dans ma poésie [...] il est rare que deux directions adverses n'y soient pas saisies ensemble, et il est vrai que je les perçois à la fois *simultanées et qui oscillent* dans la voix' ('in my poetry generally [...] it is rare that two opposite directions are not apprehended as one, and equally true that I see them as *simultaneous and oscillating to and fro* within the voice at the same moment'). He defines this phenomenon in various ways: as an 'alternance de mouvements de néantisation et d'éveil' (as 'alternating movements of annihilation and awakening') in which the linguistic self is obliterated, dies momentarily to its own words, only to be reborn, to recuperate itself, tortuously, in the processes of discourse, like a Gordian knot. Or as an elliptical dialectic such as that which polarises and give such contradictory energy and rapid mobility to the work of Rimbaud, with barely formulated perceptions impatiently pursuing each other, each superseding and annulling its predecessor in the active field of force of some ineffable, unresolved reality: 'dans la même proposition, l'affirmation, l'affirmation niée, la négation niée...' ('in one and the same proposition, the affirmation, the affirmation negated, the negation negated...'). It is as if two immeasurable orientations or virtualities of speech were coaxing and contesting each other in the same experience: hence the aspiration, frequently recurring throughout Frénaud's work, to 'joindre les deux bouches énormes l'une à l'autre' ('to join the two enormous mouths one to another'), to achieve that labial or linguistic interlocking and exchange which resembles an amorous union. Perhaps all poetry, in a sense, is just such a project: to reconcile, if only briefly and intermittently, language with its murmuring *alter ego*, be it that which stirs in the poet's head or that which lies in wait in the echoing underworld of the potential reader, and to know the momentary euphoria of discovering 'notre bouche unique' ('our single mouth').

In an important *Note sur l'expérience poétique / Note on the nature of poetic experience*, published as an adjunct to the collection *Il n'y a pas de paradis / There is no such thing as paradise*, the author gives an account of the 'mysterious event'. There is, he says, a moment when self is demolished as an obstacle, as a set of screens and filters, of self-conscious and restrictive practices, and one is drawn, perhaps in spite of oneself and for no determinable reason, into the inseparability of what he can only call 'l'Unité-du-monde-en-mouvement' ('the Unity-of-the-world-in-movement'). It is only as the poet 'reawakens' to himself – in the train or wake of a receding energy which now appears to tug words with it, dislodging them, firing them to a strange incandescence – that he strives to give it voice. The poem is born amidst the tensions and implicit contradictions stemming from the discrepancy between the 'violent va-et-vient unificateur' (the 'violent unifying to-and-fro'), and the limits of one's habitual means of expression (words with tight connotations, a reductive logic, a stiff and over-respectful syntax). It is shaped between the experience of self as other (an enlargement turned abyss in which consciousness and the world go tumbling together), and self returning to the serviceable familiarities of its own domain as self-recognition. Poetry, then, for Frénaud, falls prey to this fundamental paradox: that 'la possibilité d'exprimer ce qui le dépasse lui est donnée alors qu'il renaît comme obstacle' ('the possibility of expressing that which transcends him is granted when also he is reincarnated as obstacle'). So, the text is an equation of communication and resistance, harmonic contact and discord, fusion and separation, continuity and rupture. It is composed in the still-reverberating but now dwindling memory of the massive interference 'du *Même et de l'Autre*' ('of *Sameness and Otherness*'): an interference which translates itself simultaneously as crystallisation and loss. As Frénaud says, it is *irony* (the tension of opposites, the energy of contradiction) which motivates the poem: the poem which, while actively surmounting itself, confirms the derisory nature of its own enterprise. 'Souveraineté précaire...En prenant pied dans la conscience l'Être n'y surgit que pour disparaître', he insists ('Precarious sovereignty...Taking hold in the consciousness Being looms up only to disappear'). Is it in this respect, above all, that Rome acts as its complex parallel: an almost uncontainable constructional effort, born of an immense power transfusing time and space and then destined to withdraw, leaving its marks of potency and impotence, grandeur and ruin, articulateness and mutism?

Frénaud's work is acutely sensitive and vulnerable to parasites of the voice: the voice not 'as its own man', as it were. 'Qui parle dans cette voix? Est-ce encore une sentinelle ou déjà l'accent de l'ennemi?' ('Who speaks in that voice? Is it still a guardian on watch or already the accent of the enemy?'), he asks. The poetic process pivots indistinguishably between friendly and inimical persuasions, those to be absorbed and those to be rejected, those which reinforce and those which jeopardise, those which stay focussed on the essential and those which force a scrambling retreat, those which reach outwards towards glimpsed horizons and those which close one in again on the defensive strategies, the self-protective improvisations, the impediments and paranoias, of one's own domain. The poet speaks of 'une langue qui s'insinue dans la nôtre' ('a language which infiltrates our own'): ambivalent in itself, corroborative or subversive, supporting one's identity or picking it apart, and with which one must make compromises and agree new working equations. He calls it 'ce remuement de mots sous la langue' ('that stirring of words beneath the tongue'): a shifting sub-text which might just as easily produce the trace of a clearer sound in the voice, or a darker, more obstructed one. At one moment hinting at the strains of a 'profonde musique', it becomes at another, as it painfully, embryonically, seeks its translation, a question of 'des espèces de larves [qui] vous clappaient sous la langue' ('kinds of larvae clacking beneath your tongue'). A figurative piece with the title *Le prisonnier radieux / The radiant prisoner* presents the problem emphatically:

> Dans l'effarouchement de ma voix,
> j'ai reconnu un son plus clair.
> Ah! tu l'avais donc entendu?
> Assiégeant toujours repoussé,
> chaque nuit il te visitait.
> C'est la voix de l'autre, c'est toi.
> Sais-tu ce qu'il t'a murmuré?
> De lui tu n'auras rien de plus.

> In my voice's fit of fright
> I recognised a clearer sound
> Ah! So you heard it too?
> Ever-repulsed besieger,
> every night it called on you.
> It is the voice of otherness, it is your own.
> And what it murmured to you, can you know?
> You shall have nothing more of it.

A mere note caught in a flutter of voice, a sound so tenuous that it must tentatively invoke another listener's testimony, a communication as persistent and 'faithful' in its attentions as it is shy and parsimonious, offering and withholding, expanding self yet sealing it within its own confines: such is the nature of this strange mediation. It is not surprising that the first line of *Il n'y a pas de paradis* should read 'Je ne peux entendre la musique de l'être' ('I cannot hear the music of Being'), ousted as it is, ultimately, by 'le mur-

mure misérable du poème' ('the wretched murmur of the poem').
Nor that poetry should appear at times as a 'machine inutile',
more a clatter of loose joints and unco-ordinated parts, a contest
of notes and tones, a confusion of sound and silence: more an ill-
attuned and unstable word-pump than a well-oiled furnisher of
harmonies. In the same vein, a text called *La secrète machine* won-
ders if its laboured exertions and agonies of self-definition finally
add up to 'parure' or 'prière': superficial finery, mere verbal dress-
ing, or some viable breakthrough of spiritual energy and commu-
nication. (*La Sorcière de Rome*, it should be said, given its epic
inspiration, its far-reaching echoes of time, the great vaults of its
structure and its high-flown oratorio, comes closer, in some ways,
to apprehending 'la musique de l'être', but a music still racked by
ironies, pierced by dissonances and disrupted by silence.)

Poetry, for Frénaud, oscillates in the formative limbo of a half-
linguistic *va-et-vient*. It seeks its balance in the brief interim between
a mysterious language swelling to life and its reduction to nothing,
between an upthrust of constructional energy and its already
imminent collapse. It is not, therefore, uncommon for poetry to
bear the mark of void. 'Et déjà frémissent de puissantes paroles...
aussitôt creuses' ('And already there are potent words a-quiver...
hollow as soon as born'), one reads in *La Noce noire*. Other com-
mon images of disappearance and empty-handedness consolidate
the theme, applied unusually, however, to the mouth: 'Déjà tout
prend un air cendreux autour de toi, ma parole!' ('Already every-
thing around you has an ashy look, my word!') or 'Dans ma bouche,
du sable' ('And in my mouth there's sand'). Poetry, in this sense,
crystallises around a huge negation. It provides walls for its own
collapsing voice. Or, looked at from a slightly different perspective,
whatever walls (of structure, stanzaic form, symmetrical buttressing
or mere verbal cohesion) that it erects, these are challenged and in-
validated by the insatiable void which is both within and beyond it:
'les parois du poème cèdent,/gagnées par le Vide' ('the walls of the
poem give way,/eroded by the Void'). It celebrates, not so much a
presence as a supreme absence, insuperable, inexhaustible, which
words have only served to shape by their inability to capture it, to
outline, as it were, by default – so creating, by all that misses the
mark and perhaps as its highest achievement, the ghostly intima-
tion of that 'trône vacant dans la parole,/ imprononçable au-delà'
(that 'vacant throne in speech, the unpronounceable beyond').

It is not therefore uncommon, and is almost endemic, of a
Frénaud poem to show the strains of 'ces paroles mal capturées,

ma conquête dérisoire' ('these ill-captured words of mine and their derisory conquest'). As it is for it to register 'la nuit dans les mots' ('the darkness within words'): the impenetrable obstacle to linguistic faith. And if the poet acknowledges, in all sincerity, that 'J'ai peur de ce que j'écris' ('I am scared of what I write'), it is not in any superficial or narcissistic sense because of self-critical finickiness or fear of reader-reaction, but because of the massive mystery of what comes to usurp the voice, occupy it, divert its resources, without one knowing by what means, with what intent, nor from what unspeakable origin. It is because that 'grondement ininterrompu', the never-ending rumble, is an influence that breaks the peace and refuses to be pacified, whatever words one throws at it: the murmur which disturbs for ever, when one would prefer to be at ease with the world and with the self. To write is to be disowned, to be in exile, 'désavoués par les grandes bouches protectrices' ('disclaimed by the great protective mouths'): to be in a zone where watchwords, clichés, expressions of common currency, yes-phrases and the verbiage of conventional solidarity, can no longer offer their life-line. One is in the company of the voices of uncertainty, vulnerability and undoing: 'ces cris que nul ne borde' ('these cries which no one hems/tucks in'), all impossible containment and overspill; 'd'adverses paroles', words at loggerheads, destined to pull against each other; and linguistic gulfs which make you aware of 'du manquant dans vos mots', words with a missing dimension as their definition.

In this work, the title 'chemins du vain espoir' applies more to language and its cheated hopes than to anything else. In a passage referring to the ubiquitous displacements of 'Being', one reads: 'Qu'en garde-t-elle, ma parole transformée?/Qu'en reste-t-il dans ma vie qui a repris? [...] Plus dénué de tenir ce livre vide/où j'avais cru entendre une autre voix' ('My altered speech, what can it hold of it?/And what remains of it in my life now back on track? [...] More lacking still for holding in my hands this emptied book/in which I thought I'd heard another voice'). Indeed, in *La Sorcière*, it is not a single other voice, but a disconcerting multiplicity of voices, stirring the shadows of myth but sprung from no ascertainable mouth, which solicit one's response: voices which are not supports but so many 'rumeurs de ma fragilité' ('sounds of my fragility'), wavering signs of the problematic word-rush which prises one from oneself and fades, restoring one momentarily to the tumult only to leave one dispossessed. Frénaud writes, as perplexed victim and analyst of his own invalidated voice:

Ô dans le murmure et dans l'épaisseur de ma voix,
dénudations et recouvrements,
les divers plis de l'abîme,
quel contenu secret se blottit ou se perd!

Oh, in the murmur and the thickness of my voice,
things laid bare and things then covered up,
the folds on folds of the abyss,
what secret content huddles there or vanishes!

It is no surprise that the final words of his collection *Haeres*, lingering laconically like an epitaph and a summary, should be: '*Je balbutie – poète*' ('*I stammer – poet*'). Nor that he should, in a much earlier poem entitled *Requiescat*, generalise the image of handicapped lips, seal the bond between death and language, and invoke the compelling *mise en abyme* or reflective mirror-image of one mouth held within another, the human within the inhuman, the impotent within the omnipotent, saying: 'Entre les deux lèvres du néant,/ce si peu de bruits vagues, vite englouti' ('Between the double lips of nothingness, this modicum of dubious sound, quickly engulfed').

Given all its enemies, the construction of a poem and, on a broader scale, the construction of a book of poems, is problematical for Frénaud. 'Car quelle sorte de structure', he asks, 'ou moins rigoureusement, quelle sorte de combinaison juste et qui serait la seule possible, saurait-il découvrir à partir d'une légion de mouvements obscurs, obscurément soulevés dans le langage?' ('For what kind of structure, or less ambitiously, what kind of apt combination which would be the only one possible, could he possibly arrive at on the basis of a multitude of obscure movements, obscurely summoned up in language?') For poetry belongs to the intersection. It is, one might say (touching again on the symbolic value of Rome), 'à la croix': caught in the never-ending upheaval between human reality and the potent notion of being. It is not a sanctuary (though it holds some sense of the sacred), but a tentative and provisional structure built on the fluctuations of a massive disturbance. The dream of the 'château' becomes a haunting motif in Frénaud's work. It represents an inaccessible 'château de l'âme', a kind of fortress of the spirit, somewhere beyond the self-searching, the contradictions, the relapses and undoings. But it is also the recurring glimpse, during the tortuous journey of literary creation (with its intermittent phases, back-tracks and crossed paths), of the ideal of accomplished form and the perfect haven of arrival: 'c'est, en cours de route, le poème comme finalité rêvée' ('It is the poem, while still on its journey, seen as a dreamed-of finality'). There is a dialectic contest between 'se fonder' and 'se fondre', between 'to found' and 'to confound', so to speak (words which, in their anagrammatic mirroring, seem to interlock as one inseparable truth): between all that seeks to stabilise and establish and all that conspires to dissolve and disperse, between fusion and confusion. The tensions of structure and collapse, of the edifice and the erosion, are captured in the following question, uttered amidst a Hieronymus Bosch-like vision of disorientated parts and mutilated limbs, in *Miroir de l'homme par les bêtes / The mirror of man via the beasts*: 'Saurons-nous déchiffrer la partition/sur la tourelle dévastée?' ('Will we manage to decipher the score/from this turret in ruins?').

Frénaud has made a series of revealing comments on the creative formation and global structure of *La Sorcière de Rome*. Despite its fifteen echoing movements supporting each other like cathedral architecture, its deep celebratory resonances, and the complex musical rhetoric of its many-layered and richly ornamented oratorio, its musical score is not, nor ever was in its original conception, in any way coherent, orderly or easily interpretable. On the contrary, the poet charts a bewildering process of irruption and interruption: of a sudden preliminary surge moulding itself obscurely into a 'massif verbal', then succeeded by innumerable breaks, hesitations, tentative engagements and re-engagements over the course of time with what has by now become a demanding presence, not a mere outcrop but a major upheaval in the malleable geography of words-in-the-mind. He speaks particularly of how, in his case, this massif or 'primitive magma', as he calls it, frequently breaks into two as an emphatic beginning and an end to a text as yet ignorant of its formative and interrelational possibilities. He compares the process in some way to the operation of dreams, in the sense that the realisation of desire is vaguely foreshadowed and already anticipated from the outset, but then submerged by the constructional activities of dreams themselves as they invent paths, probable or improbable, masked or more or less patent, towards it. More precisely, in these first stages, the poem, in seeming to discover intuitively its first and last words, appears to be marking out or putting in place 'pour s'y enfouir l'orifice dont il est sorti' ('so that it may re-bury itself, the very orifice it has emerged from'). In the beginning is the word, one might say, and in the word is its own beginning and end. The alpha and omega are conjoined in the first energetic outburst of poetic utterance. (The first words of *La Sorcière* refer to 'secret voices', heard or unheard, and the last to a problematical 'mouthpiece of truth', more or less clouded. These are the extreme poles of the text: a mouth which initiates and a mouth which closes, a mouth which in initiating closes, and which in closing initiates. Such a circular structure creates the field of attraction to make one not only aware of, but susceptible as reader to, the desire to 'joindre les deux bouches énormes'.) Applying a more concrete explanatory image, Frénaud says: 'le poème va progresser à la façon d'un grand serpent qui formera un cercle, non sans méandres inutiles, voies de traverse, peaux tombées, pour retourner se mordre la queue. Nouvelle image d'un éternel retour du même' ('the poem will advance like some great snake circling round, though not without fruitless meanderings, shortcuts here and there and cast off skins, to reach back and bite its own tail. Yet another image of the eternal return of the same'). He then brings a further perspective to bear: that of the void or turbulence at the centre of the poem, of the unfathomable gulf between its two walls. 'Oui, il ne restera plus au poème qu'à venir se loger dans l'emplacement vide entre ses deux bords!' he writes,

> Cela paraît un abîme! [...] Ou, si l'on veut, il y aura un frémissement imperceptible dans l'arrière-gorge, qui durera jusqu'à l'achèvement. Il m'est arrivé souvent d'avoir l'impression comme d'une boule qui n'en finit pas de tourner – on m'a dit, une fois, que c'était la boule hystérique – englobant tous les sons et tous les sens, bruissement énorme d'où se détacheraient soudain des agglutinations verbales, bribes du poème.

> Yes, all that remains for the poem to do is to take up its place in the empty arena between the two edges! A space like an abyss! [...] Or, to put it another way, an imperceptible quivering will occur in the back of the throat lasting until the text is complete. I have often had the impression of a kind of ball endlessly spinning – someone once said it was the ball of hysteria – entwining every sound and every sense, immeasurable murmur suddenly breaking off from which come verbal conglomerations, snatches of the poem.

The Witch or Sorceress is, among many other things, the 'boule hystérique' at the heart of language, the twirling, humming matrix of all sound and sense: the feverish, elusive patroness of the verbal abyss.

Any reading of *La Sorcière de Rome* and of what happens between its walls, within the ambitions of its own structural citadel, so to speak, will reveal the ravages of a language of deconstruction. From the beginning, one is aware of multi-directional words, caught between roman and italics; of fragments of 'dead language' momentarily brought to life; of the precarious dialogues of intertextuality, with more lacunae than links; of speech from unattributable sources creating dangerous encounters; of a profuse unsifted sign-language slipping beyond the grids of interpretation; of voices which 'carry' (across time and space, laden with unidentified cargoes) only to break off and renounce communication. One sees how the material of language gapes, splinters into uneven shapes, loses its footing in its own progression, lurches from dimension to dimension (between self and city, present and past, private and public). Messages are caught and lost, make the subconscious bristle and vanish. The syntax does itself violence, at times fully fashioned, at times left verbless, truncated or hanging in mid-air: the victim of its crucifixion between conduction and resistance. Bundles of questions, hastily grasped and assembled, tie and untie the text. One advances by detours, groping in a linguistic *clair-obscur* (hovering between abstract and concrete, figurative and literal, portentous and colloquial, rational and irrational, coherent and frantically associative). Language issues warnings against itself. It is its own worst enemy: a counterpoint of contradictions, a meeting-point of irresolutions. Frénaud describes his own poems, and especially the extended or epic ones which allow a further-reaching apprehension of the frustrations of the quest, as 'ces constructions verbales de dimension souvent vaste, avec des raccourcis et des ruptures, des raccordements imprévus, tous les bouleversements d'une longue phrase qui tâche de s'y retrouver et de s'inventer une certaine unité' ('these verbal constructions of often considerable dimension, with things curtailed and cut off, unexpected reconnections, and all the disruptions of a long poetic phrase seeking to find its way and create for itself a kind of unity'). And within that linguistic quest, one is never far from what, in *Les portes bleues* (a title which applies as much as anything to the dreamed-of celestial openings in the word), he refers to as 'un buissonnement de signes en quête d'une réalité qu'ils semblaient vouloir saisir ou reconnaître: gribouillis et racines, bribes de grimoire, approximations incompréhensibles, passionnées, mots de passe peu déchiffrables, tout un balbutiement mortel pour trouver un accès' ('a thicket of signs in search of a reality they seemed to yearn to grasp or recognise: scribblings and root-sprouts, scrawlings of magic spells, incomprehensible, impassioned approximations, scarcely decipherable pass-words, a whole stammering of human mortality trying to find access').

If, then, Frénaud has said, 'Le poème doit être hérissé, ocellé,/ incessamment tressaillir' ('The poem must be bristling, luminously rippling/endlessly quivering'), then *La Sorcière de Rome*, as an epic but an unfinished or flawed epic (a 'voix fêlée') which, of necessity, can never complete its own grandeur, must be seen as a supreme example. And none other of his poems better exemplifies the force of his statement: 'Dans l'enclosure du poème se joue l'abîme' ('Mockingly, in the poem's enclosure, moves the abyss').

The Poem in the Mirror

The proof that *La Sorcière de Rome* could not close definitely on itself is the long series of *Gloses* or explanatory glosses on the text elaborated by Frénaud since the 'completion' of the poem at the end of 1969, and which he was still continuing up to the time of his death in 1993. Such glosses have been published on Movements 1, 3, 4, 5, 11, 12 and 13, and reveal the extent to which *La Sorcière* has had its own demanding and extensive underground life. It has journeyed through time, still unsure of its destination and meaning. It has sought new translations, in a prosaic language perhaps complementary to the poetic one, perhaps inimical to it: fusing and parting, illuminating and obscuring, correcting and warping, corroborating and betraying – but, in all events, conjuring up new and searching dialogues, more crossroads of the voice. It has resurrected itself again and again as a potent generative source, no less so than the voice of the dead as evoked in *Les morts et la parole*:

> Il y a ce qui pourrit, ce qui cède ou s'abandonne
> et peut renaître après une randonnée par l'obscur.
> L'oreille entend, de telle bouche neuve,
> un vocable germer d'une racine qu'on croyait vide.
> Enorme parturition murmurante.
> Les morts, en vérité, ne respirent que par nous,
> donateurs du commun langage, bâtisseurs
> d'édifices que tu conserves dans la gorge.

> And then there is what rots, what yields, relinquishes itself
> and still can be reborn after a journey through the dark.
> The ear can hear, from this or that new mouth,
> the sprouting of a term from roots one thought played out.
> Immeasurable murmurings of birth.
> Indeed, the dead breathe only via us,
> our gift of common language, builders
> of massive structures you preserve inside your throat.

The structure of *La Sorcière*, already one of the longest and most intricate poems in Frénaud's poetic landscape, has led to the building of enormous annexes and secondary crypts modelled on the original, designed to explain the mysteries in another tongue, and perhaps to another readership. It fulfils, in this sense, the sort of structural multiplication or *mise en abyme* (reflections beyond reflections) seen by the poet and critic in his reading of a painting by Mantegna:

> Et l'architecture du tableau contribue à nous entraîner au-delà de ce qu'il représente. Ces arcs, ces escaliers et ces colonnes, ces places, ces maisons qui s'éloignent si magnifiquement sont disposés de telle sorte qu'ils appellent d'autres arcs et des colonnes et des escaliers et d'autres places à n'en plus finir, et celui qui regarde n'est pas plus assuré d'atteindre ce qu'il cherche que l'arpenteur de Kafka quand il examinait le *Château*.

> And the architecture of the painting helps to draw us beyond what it actually depicts. These arches, stairways and columns, these *piazzas*, these houses receding so magnificently into the distance are arranged in such a way as to invoke other arches and columns and stairways and other *piazzas* endlessly, and the spectator is no more guaranteed to reach what he seeks than was Kafka's surveyor in examining the *Castle*.

The *Gloses*, then, though couched in a more analytical, expository language, represent and are the product of all that is *insaisissable* – virtual, imminent, obscurely metaphorical, linguistically elusive, over-elliptical, rapidly self-erasing – in the heart of the original text. So, just as Frénaud, *in* the poem, has gone back through time to the mysteries of Rome, the fount of Western civilisation, with its latent voices and its scattered sign-language, in order to fathom its dubious hold on our psychology, its multifarious influences, its hidden relationships through myth, so, *after* the poem, he has gone back through time to *its* signs, images and inscriptions, *its* multiple and divergent voices and *its* broken architecture, in order to explore again, with different instruments and different perspectives, *this* great fount of poetic words (a monumental configuration in its own right) which has by no means divulged all its secrets or exhausted its mysteries. Rome as a great dark matrix is matched by the poem as a great dark matrix. They are in each other's image. Both have seen a powerful *événement* with its prolonged aftermath. Both represent a disturbance and an exaltation followed by a long history of inconclusive interpretation.

In *Le Château et la quête du poème* (and it is perhaps the quest of the poem which, for him, ultimately subsumes all others), Frénaud describes how, in the poetic act, there is an experience of the self made other and the self restored to itself as self-recognition. This is translated in the partial opaqueness, impenetrability and seeming inadequacy of the poetic object which the 'author' must confront, with some perplexity, on his 'return', so to speak:

43

Et la fulguration évanouie, il ne restera qu'un monument en face de lui, plus ou moins ample et élevé, dont il fera le tour avec déception [...] Et il s'efforcera de retrouver, à l'examiner de différents côtés, à y monter et descendre, à parcourir salles et corridors, à se fixer tout à coup sur telle arête fuyante, au défaut des proportions et des formes, quelques échos de la voix illuminante qui s'est fait entendre, parfois, au cours et au sommet de la route.

And once the dazzling illumination has vanished, all that will be left before him is a monument, more or less ample and lofty, which he will proceed to survey from different angles with some disenchantment [...] And he will seek to rediscover there, examining it from all sides, climbing to the top and down again, scouring its rooms and corridors, halting suddenly on this or that receding ridge, for want of more stable proportions and forms, a few echoes of the enlightening voice which had made itself heard, intermittently, along and on the crest of the road he had travelled.

La Sorcière is, indeed, one of the most 'ample and lofty' of the poet's monuments. And the process of 'examining it from all sides' is proportionately vast. The *Gloses* probe its hidden corridors, unearth new secret passageways, test structural joints and weak-spots, investigate signs, confront arresting images, cast light on the fleeting and underdeveloped, expand the laconic, give voice to the receding voices, re-layer the echoes. They are essential reading for anyone who wishes to delve fully into the richness of *La Sorcière*'s 'double life' (only curtailed by the author's death).

The *Gloses* represent another way of bringing together the alpha and the omega: the original poetic surge, forward-thrusting, tentative, unsure of its directions, obscurely turbulent; and more considered reflection on its end-product, its prolonged but subsiding after-shocks, as it were, now more amenable to measured readings (perhaps all the more erroneous for that very reason) and to the retrospective interpretation. The alpha and omega, however, which only join to form a circle round a mystery – or, might one say, male and female clasping each other to create a textual abyss of love, now enlarged and even more compelling or vertiginous: the text making love to itself, seeking its own union and totality through time and space. Frénaud, as we have seen, returns time and again to the shadowy attractions of 'la grande matrice nocturne' ('the great dark matrix'): indeed, the Sorceress is nothing other. The *Gloses* go back upstream, now to a double Sorceress, approaching her through a double screen or thickness: the original anonymous force of history, myth or legend which first sucked in the poem before a word was spoken, and her latest reincarnation in that textual face or tinted verbal mask which bears the name *La Sorcière de Rome.* The author's final published volume of poetry, *Nul ne s'égare / No one goes astray*, ends with a complex polyphonic poem entitled *Comme un serpent remonte les rivières / As a snake goes back upstream.* It is a poem largely composed, in a tortuous, snaking way, with insecure threads slipping underground temporarily and resurfacing, of brief extracts or quotations from his own work, emerging unpredictably from various collections stretching through time. It is, therefore, a fluid though disrupted journey back to the vast genetic source, through the problematic ripples of relationships, the hazards of memory, the selective filters of association: back into the deepest reaches of his own poetic creativity, however clouded or fragmentary. At the same time, it is a journey forward, resurrecting pieces of the past, as if to prove, Bergson-fashion, that their life is not spent, not sealed for ever behind the walled-up windows of the published book or the superseded self, but available for a new poetic venture, given a future, carried elsewhere, enlisted into unseen combinations, and able to re-fertilise beyond their originally imposed, provisional boundaries of time, text and self. The *Gloses* fulfil a not dissimilar function. They are an enormous enterprise of genetic criticism. Words used to comment on *Comme un serpent...* apply equally well to them: they are written, says Frénaud, 'pour tâcher de reconnaître [...] les forces souterraines qui vont se structurant dans ma poésie' ('to seek to recognise [...] the underground forces which conspire to shape their structures in my poetry'). He makes explicit, in the Pingaud dialogue of 1977, by which date they had already been undertaken, that they are an expression of his fascination with the obscure origins and complex birth-processes of the poetic text:

> Il me faudrait une fois donner un exemple du travail du poème, en analysant au microscope, d'après mes notes au jour le jour, la généalogie d'un d'eux. J'ai commencé et interrompu un volume de *Gloses à la Sorcière* qui risque d'être interminable...

> I really must at some moment give an illustration of the workings of the poem, analysing microscopically, from my day-by-day annotations, the genealogy of one of them. I have begun and temporarily suspended a volume of *Glosses on the Sorceress* which runs the risk of becoming never-ending...

And, like *Comme un serpent...* (and perhaps like any committed act of literary criticism), they go upstream and downstream at the same time: back towards the profuse well-springs which first produced this, the most enigmatic and richly interrelational of Frénaud's texts; and forwards, on the flood of sources reopened, into new

45

patterns and elucidations which enlarge that text, carry it further than it could have known and reawaken it to its second life: the *Gloses* as an immeasurable *alter ego*, as it were, still spilling and finding unforeseeable new channels, long after the main lock-gates have been assumed to have closed.

The title *Haeres* sits obscurely at the centre of the problem of literary heritage or inheritance which pervades Frénaud's work. It is a problem which assumes many dimensions: not only that of one's ambivalent relationship of indebtedness and revolt with mother or father figures, or of psychological, religious or cultural influences handed down by various circuitous routes from the historical patronage of Rome, but, more especially in this context, of the created literary text itself and the hold it has on one, the bonds it creates with a receptive or resistant psyche, the prerogatives it continues to exercise through its prejudicial models, its implants in one's language, its parcels of self already imprisoned or usurped, its half-heard voices impinging from beyond the grave. In what ways is the author his own inheritor? The *Gloses*, indeed, are the bewildered inheritor of *La Sorcière*. They take up the responsibility and the challenge, the unknowns and apparent incompatibilities, the ambiguity and the problematical tensions, the 'black holes' and unchecked disturbances, of its strange textual legacy. For, if it is true, as Frénaud says, that

> Il y a, au cœur du poème, derrière le poème, révélé par lui, un magma de multiples forces contraires, qui tournent, s'entrecroisent, se heurtent, veulent s'échapper...Et qui s'échappent, effectivement, en propos obscurs – ce sera le poème – sans ordre apparent, possiblement

> In the heart of the poem, behind the poem, revealed by it, lies a magma of opposite forces in abundance, which twist and turn, criss-cross, clash, seek to escape...And which do escape, indeed, in obscure verbalisations – which will be the poem – in no apparent logical order, conceivably

then the author can in no way have exhausted the momentum, let alone drained the significance, of that insatiable Eros-in-the-word. It has agreed to form a mouth, it has borrowed another mouthpiece, however constricted or convoluted in structure. And that mouthpiece may well allow re-entry, and new intimations, after the event, of the violent momentary accord which locked together world and self and decomposed them both, in order to make them available, paradoxically, to the searching compositional enterprises of the poetic word. It is such a re-entry that is sought, tried and retried, movement by movement, by the long history of the *Gloses*. As the author explains:

Sans doute, à reprendre le poème dans sa voix, l'auteur a-t-il la chance, une fois ou l'autre, sinon de s'abîmer à nouveau dans la grande néantisation brouillonnante et sacrée, du moins d'en renouveler, si peu que ce soit, le bouillonnement – les balbutiements – avec cette impression de transcendance qu'il donne. C'est donc qu'il peut demeurer quelque pouvoir exorbitant dans l'objet refroidi

And no doubt the author, in taking the poem back in his mouth, has the chance, on some occasion or another, if not to plunge again into that great sacred, confused and unsystematic annihilation of things, then at least to revive, if only minimally, its seething presence – its stammerings – and the impression of transcendence that goes with it. Proof, therefore, that some inordinate force can live on in the object now in its cooled down state.

The poem, then, is the author's only ascertainable heritage, 'transmissible de soi à soi' ('transmissible from oneself to oneself'): something once accumulated from unclear sources, perhaps half-forgotten, even sealed away, but waiting to be passed on (with the apparent death of a self) as an unexpected fund, swollen with interest, which will afford new expansive possibilities, even a resurrection and a proof of immortality. It is in this sense that one can return to the statement: 'Où est mon pays? C'est dans le poème'. For there, and not in Rome (which is no more than its agent), and certainly not in any more religious notion of an 'afterlife', he rediscovers, repeatedly, 'un écho de la patrie véritable' ('an echo of the true homeland'): that is to say, the vast domain where self hears self, pasts and presents commune, and one comes to an enhanced understanding of what constitutes the indestructible, still evolving totality of one's being through time.

The *Gloses* also demonstrate that the self is inexhaustible and irreducible. Their multiplication of approaches, their plurality of readings, their reworkings of interpretations, their sounding of undersides, their exploration of alternatives, their tentative forays through defences and masks into protected zones and subconscious obscurities, go to prove, as Frénaud says, that 'Je est légion, il est champ de bataille, automystification, lieu de tromperie' ('I is legion, it is battlefield, self-delusion, place of deceits'). They are a revisiting of his battlefield, where he is both the ally and the enemy. They are a place of almost bottomless self-interrogation, where he can over-indulge that drug-like 'démon autocritique' ('demon of self-criticism') which stems from and incessantly aggravates the realisation that 'Je me suis inacceptable' ('I am unacceptable to myself '), the knowledge that one always has some self-refusal and non-recognition in reserve. They are a mirror and an abyss, for the captivated Narcissus. As he writes in *Saurons-nous cesser d'enterrer les morts?* / *Will we ever stop burying the dead?*:

> La stoïque allure que prend Narcisse,
> comme elle me plaît!
> Oserai-je me retrouver naïf encore
> en ces miroirs,
> où déjà s'éparpillent silhouettes brouillées,
> soupirs goguenards, grimaces?

> The stoic bearing assumed by Narcissus,
> how it appeals to me!
> Dare I rediscover me still as first innocence
> amidst these mirrors,
> where are scattered already blurred images,
> mocking wisps of voice and grimaces?

They are a form of confession, long overdue, one might say, spoken in the huge baroque confessional box and its surrounding structure which is *La Sorcière de Rome*. But a confession, now never-ending, thickened with countless layers of experience and self-awareness, which blurs the issue and drowns one in tumbling echoes. The self is not subdued. It is not back in the fold. And if the *Gloses* adopt, among their many shifting tones and critical registers, an intimate confessional mode, it is not to unite the self with the self and to find comforting or comfortable reconciliation, but, in the end, to expose new dimensions of division and perplexing confrontation – as this further acknowledgement from *Will we ever stop burying the dead?* indicates: 'J'ai envie de me confesser, sans père ni mère [...] Mon seul témoin c'est moi, témoin qui raille' ('I want to confess, without father or mother [...] My only witness is me, witness with the mocking voice'). The bringing together of *La Sorcière* and the *Gloses*, the church and its unfinished flying buttresses, is a massive meeting of the man and himself. There could be no more emphatic illustration that the self goes far beyond its legible significances, that it is prolific in feeding its own doubles, that it is an eternal rebel to itself, and that, even in death, it is not yet ready to be consigned to the tomb or any similar one container.

The *Gloses*, finally, are the proof that one has not subdued *La Sorcière* (book or person, text or spirit). One has not imprisoned her and all that she represents in a 'monument of stone'. Words will go back, time and time again, to the mysteries of the crypt, to raise the lid, to let out, together with the groan of tragic man, the secret odours of the nameless.

PETER BROOME
Queen's University, Belfast

Selected Bibliography

ANDRÉ FRÉNAUD: Major works

Dates in brackets after a title indicate the first date of publication of an edition of that work. All titles are collections of poetry except where otherwise stated.

Les Rois Mages (1943) suivi de *L'Étape dans la clairière* (1966) et de *Pour une plus haute flamme par le défi* (Gallimard, Collection Poésie, 1987).

Il n'y a pas de paradis (1962) (Gallimard, Collection Poésie, 1967)

La Sainte Face (1968) (Gallimard, Collection Poésie, 1986).

La Sorcière de Rome (1973) suivi de *Depuis toujours déjà* (1970) (Gallimard, Collection Poésie, 1984).

Notre inhabileté fatale: interviews with Bernard Pingaud (Gallimard, 1979).

Haeres (Gallimard, 1982).

Ubac et les fondements de son art: essays on the painter and sculptor (Adrien Maeght, 1985).

Nul ne s'égare (Gallimard, 1986).

Gloses à la Sorcière: prose commentaries, edited and introduced by Bernard Pingaud (Gallimard, 1995).

ANDRÉ FRÉNAUD: English Translations

A Round O, translated by Keith Bosley (London: Interim Press, 1977).

November, translated by John Montague (Cork: The Golden Stone, 1977).

ANDRÉ FRÉNAUD: Further Reading

Georges-Emmanuel Clancier: *André Frénaud* (Seghers, Poètes d'aujourd'hui 37, 1963).

Sud: André Frénaud, Vol. XI, Nos. 39-40, 1981.

Sud: Frénaud-Tardieu, Vol. XIV, Nos. 50-51, 1984.

Lire Frénaud (Presses universitaires de Lyon, 1985).

La Quinzaine Littéraire, No. 455, 16-31 January 1986.

Alain Suied: *André Frénaud: poète ontologique* (Dominique Bedou, 1986).

Peter Broome: *André Frénaud* (Rodopi, 1986).

La Nouvelle Revue Française, No. 430 (November 1988).

Roger Little: *André Frénaud entre l'interrogation et le vide* (Sud, 1989).

Jean-Yves Debreuille, *André Frénaud* (Seghers, Poètes d'aujourd'hui 261), 1989.

Europe, Nos. 734-35, 1990.

Roger Munier: *L'Être et son poème: essai sur la poétique d'André Frénaud* (Encres Marines, Fougères, 1993).

Pour André Frénaud (Obsidiane/Le Temps qu'il fait, 1993).

Rome the Sorceress

La Sorcière de Rome

Amne perenne latens, Anna Perenna vocor
OVIDE
Fastes, III 654

Ne ricanent pas les colombes, et le tigre ne lèche.

Qui l'a dit?
Laisse venir les signes qui s'ouvrent au-dessous.
Laisse affluer
toutes figures affrontées dans la parole.

Hid by the permanent stream, Anna Perenna I'm called
OVID
Fasti, III 654

Doves do not sneer, and the tiger does not lick.

Who said that?
Let the signs come that open underneath.
Let all
insulted faces flow into speech.

[I]

La vieille entendra-t-elle ces voix secrètes?
Les conduits se répercutaient le bruit profond.
Qui gémit? Qui conspire? Qui retient les torrents?
Des bêtes affamées sont dans les ruelles,
rongent les auges ténébreuses.

Nous, derrière les remparts, mal assurés,
sur les escaliers dressés par la hauteur,
pour regarder le monde étalé sur l'autre pente,
notre pouvoir au soleil chaleureux, pour nous réjouir
d'une cité apparue dans ses feuillages.

– Des jeunes gens sourient là-bas, ils s'embrassent.
Un petit âne monte les marches, le faix
s'accroche à la colonne et tombe.

– Pourquoi surgissent, dans notre citadelle, des fumées
qui se glissent à travers les dalles, s'éloignent?
Le ciel est clair et les dômes, de proche en proche,
tiennent en ordre les quartiers.
Les déesses marchent, assurées, dans le jardin précieux.
Des fontaines jouent. Entrepôts qui regorgent. Partout
l'abondance à tout pourrir et des rats.

[I]

Will the old woman hear those secret voices?
The ducts were knocking with the noise from the deep.
Who is groaning, plotting, holding back the flood?
Hungry beasts are in the alleyways,
gnawing at the troughs in the dark.

We, behind the ramparts, uncertain,
upon the many stairs raised by ambition,
to look at the world laid out on the other slope,
our power in the warm sun, to rejoice
in a city glimpsed through its foliage.

– Young people are smiling there, are kissing.
A little donkey is climbing the steps, its load
catches on the column and falls.

– Why in our citadel is smoke rising,
slipping across the flagstones, sliding away?
The sky is clear and the domes in their degrees
keep the districts in order.
The goddesses walk with confidence in the precious garden.
Fountains play. Warehouses overflowing. Everywhere
abundance till it rots, and rats.

Depuis toujours la gloire et, plus l'on creuse, la gloire,
égarée dans ses éboulis.
Et plus l'on monte, plus l'on se hausse
pour s'égaler et pour confondre.
Et tout haut fait est, à mesure, commémoré.
Et la Croix, encore un coup, irradiera au faîte.
Les demeures se rengorgent de voûte en voûte
et de colline à colline. Les plafonds
se sont couverts de mouvements de majesté.
Les miroirs, en abîme, assujettissent la splendeur.

Assez de tes éloges sur les arcs triomphaux,
DUX, PONTIFEX IMPERATOR.
Assez de marches pour vous hausser, assez
d'inscriptions déchiffrables.
De la ruine d'un four à pain s'extirpant, le grillon
module de sa voix maigre, de père en fils,
le même cri anonyme.
Et le grand tout, depuis toujours son mouvement
nous emporte au-delà des gestes mémorables –
à travers le cortège immobile des marbres,
impatients dans la rumeur.

Serait-ce l'addition ultime, la somme,
le sommet gagné décidément, l'insaisissable
couronne irradiant, l'hymne avec la bénédiction?

– Tant de fois brûlées, les archives
retrouvées plus antiques sont là terribles,
leur fumée pèse…Un soleil de marbre nous éblouit.

Glory from the beginning, glory the deeper we dig,
glory in strewn rubble.
And the higher we climb, the higher we push
to draw level and merge.
And each height reached is one by one recorded.
And the Cross, once again, will shine forth at the peak.
Dwellings parade from vault to vault
from hill to hill. Ceilings
are clouded over with majestic progress.
Unfathomable mirrors subdue the splendour.

Enough of your praises on triumphal arches,
DUX, PONTIFEX IMPERATOR.
Enough of steps to raise yourselves, enough
of inscriptions we can read.
Extracting itself from the ruin of a baker's oven,
the thin-voiced cricket intones from father to son
the same nameless cry.
And the great All, its movement from the beginning
bears us away beyond memorable gestures –
across the marbles' motionless procession,
impatient amid uproar.

Would this be the final accretion, the sum,
the summit decidedly reached, the ungraspable
crown shining forth, the hymn with the blessing?

– So many times burnt, the archives
found again to be more ancient are terrible there,
their smoke hangs... A marble sun dazzles us.

[II]

ENFOUIE DANS LE FLEUVE DEPUIS TOUJOURS EN MARCHE,
ENFIN LA GRANDE, L'INNOMBRABLE, SE RASSEMBLE
ET SE CHERCHE UN VISAGE, SE FORME
PAROLE PAR LE GRONDEMENT, SOUDAIN M'INONDE,
M'ILLUMINA,
            QUAND DESSAISI,
JE LA RECONNUS DANS MA VOIX
                        TOUTE PRÉSENCE,
UN SEUL AVEC ELLE, ÉVANOUI.

Je renaissais. Suis séparé,...j'essaie d'entendre.

...Non tu n'es pas, Rome,
pénétration de l'abîme et soleil qui monte,
l'aigle éternel dans sa gravitation,
ni l'épreuve et la preuve
d'un avènement promis décisif,
mais rien qu'un regard sur le triomphal avec
une suite à découvrir et recouvrer,
une voix sans fin éperdue, qui sait,
qui ne sait pas, qu'on interroge.

Que trouvions-nous marqué, que nous sachions lire?
Que se trouve-t-il masqué, que nous ne saurons dire?
Qui se terre, qui doit se taire?

60

[II]

CONCEALED IN THE RIVER FLOWING FROM THE BEGINNING,
AT LAST THE GREAT BEYOND RECKONING GATHERS HERSELF
AND SEEKS A FACE FOR HERSELF, FORMS FOR HERSELF
SPEECH BY RUMBLING, SUDDENLY OVERWHELMS ME,
LIT ME,
   WHEN DISPOSSESSED,
I RECOGNISED IN MY VOICE
      ALL OF HER,
ONE ALONE WITH HER AND ASWOON.

I was being reborn. Am separate,... I try to hear.

...No you are not, Rome,
entry into the abyss and rising sun,
the eagle eternal in its gravitation,
nor trial and token
of a promised accession that resolves,
but a mere glance upon the triumphal with
a sequel to be discovered and retrieved,
a voice endlessly bewildered, that knows,
does not know, is questioned.

What did we find marked out that could be read?
What's masked that by us never can be said?
Who goes to ground who must make no sound?

[III]

...Qui n'oublierait cette voix dans la rue enjouée,
si le soleil du matin flâne par la ville?
Allegria.

Pied de marbre géant, conservé sans nul corps
en statue pour nous divertir, tortue
porteuse du monde, éléphant sous sa colonne,
petit enfant joueur... Et terrasse tendre,
avec le géranium embaumant
l'antique tombeau élogieux,
la lente fontaine qui s'élève, le murmure
de vasque en vasque entre les escaliers,
entre les statues qu'on voit au bout du ciel,
une tourterelle et un *fiasco* sur la marche.

Qui a voulu
des fragments de colline et la beauté des portes
en ce palais? Qui a voulu
les nuits exposées aux bêtes en ce palais?
Je me souviens: un abîme sur le bord de la route,
près du figuier. Puis il y eut
foisonnement d'animaux qui s'empoignent,
de longs corps blancs dans la boue, le dos qui étincelle,
une chevelure...Serait-ce là? J'ai tant rêvé.

...Il faut bâtir des palais pour occuper les pauvres.
Pour les divertir d'eux et nous en protéger.
La blancheur des vestales brûle aux petits couvents.
Les esclaves châtrés sur le parvis
de la Fortune Virile. Tel est l'Ordre.
Ne bâille pas. Nous irons jouir
dans les temples comme dans les égouts.

[III]

...Who would not forget that voice in the playful street,
if the morning sun strolls through the town?
Allegria.

A giant marble foot, preserved with no body
as a statue to amuse us, a tortoise
bearing the world, an elephant beneath its column,
a small child playing... And a tender terrace,
embalming with geranium
the ancient laudatory tomb,
the slow fountain rising, the whisper
from basin to basin between the stairways,
between the statues seen at the sky's end,
a turtle-dove and a *fiasco* on the step.

Who wanted
fragments of hill and the beauty of gates
in this palace? Who wanted
nights exposed to beasts in this palace?
I remember: a pit at the roadside,
near the fig tree. Then there was
a glut of animals laying hold of one another,
long white bodies in the mud, the glistening back,
someone's hair...Would it be there? I have dreamed so much.

...Palaces must be built to keep the poor busy.
To distract them from themselves and protect ourselves from them.
The vestals' whiteness burns in the small convents.
The castrated slaves in the courtyard
of Fortuna Virilis. Such is Order.
Don't yawn. We shall go to have fun
in temples as in sewers.

...Caresses d'or, poses toutes plus belles
pour capter l'autre ou plaire à soi.
Tumultes sans savoir et grands gestes pour taire.
Figures affrontées qui savez vous ouvrir
au plaisir et passez. Face éclatante, obscure.
Parades sans avoir, les cœurs parés.

Les corps traversés, la mêlée, l'extase,
l'innombrable éclair saisi dans la traînée des cris.
Puis le dénuement tout à coup, l'opaque.

Grande nourricière, si tu sais mon désir,
laisseras-tu passer paroles qui m'éclairent?

...Golden caresses, postures all more beautiful
for picking up the other or pleasing oneself.
Unknowing tumults and big gestures to shut up.
Insulted faces, you who know how to open
to pleasure and then pass. Flashing, dark aspect.
Parades without possession, hearts adorned.

Bodies gone through, confusion, ecstasy,
the unnumbered flash seized in the trail of cries.
Then the sudden stripping, the opaque.

Great foster mother, if you know what I want,
would you let slip words to enlighten me?

[IV]

Qui se cache?
Mais qui parle?
Qui s'accroît, qui s'inscrit par la nuit pour surgir
des entrepôts du ventre?
Qui s'investit? Qui procède au recouvrement?

L'antique noyée qui s'éveille au printemps,
avide et se donne, la riche veuve
qui rend ses greniers aux mains de l'insatisfait,
une autre, plus pâle, dans une grotte avec des prêtres,
pour l'aider à se délivrer de sa parole,
et c'est toujours la même qui s'échappe
de la coulée inlassable noire,
comme du lait gicle de la Nuit,
gardant nostalgie d'une torpeur initiale
qui se retrouve menace devant soi.

Toute créature passe
par une eau obscure avant de naître.
Sortie de là, tous les pas qu'elle fait
la rapprochent du plus noir... Les mêmes,
elle voudrait qu'ils la détournent,
à défaut de l'éloigner, l'en distraient.
La tendresse un instant crée l'infini.
Les serpents du délire, leur explosion cruelle
force l'ouverture, et le temps s'abîma.
S'échapper...Être épris...Mais nous sommes là tous,
besognant le parcours.

Tu hurlais, allant à ton supplice, grande vestale,
qui tentas de trouver objet d'amour ici,
à l'encontre d'un vœu qu'on te fit prononcer
pour établir notre sauvegarde,
et fus pour ce péché enterrée vive.
Le rappel bien trouvé de notre sort bouffon:
sortis d'une tombe pour y retomber!

[IV]

Who is hiding?
          But who is speaking?
Who grows, who writes his name by night to emerge
from the stores of the belly?
Who invests himself? Who proceeds to recovery?

The woman drowned long since who wakes to the spring,
eager, and gives herself, the rich widow
who delivers her granaries into dissatisfied hands,
another woman, paler, in a cave with priests,
to help her release herself from her word,
and always the same one gets away
from the black ceaseless outflow,
as milk squirts from Night,
sadly recalling an early sluggishness
that once more poses a threat.

Every creature passes
through a dark water before birth.
Once out of there, all the steps it takes
bring it close to something darker...The same steps,
it would like them to turn it away,
if they cannot remove it, then to distract it.
Tenderness for a moment creates the infinite.
The snakes of delirium, their cruel explosion
forces the opening, and time was ruined.
To escape...To be in love... But we are all there,
labouring the course.

You howled on your way to be tortured, great vestal,
who tried to find here something you could love,
defying a vow you were required to take
to establish our safe keeping,
and were for this sin buried alive.
The well-found reminder of our comical fate:
out of a tomb only to fall back in!

...La mort ne se tait pas dans cette voix haineuse,
où elle n'est pas seule à rêver et maudire.
Si la vie est recours contre son terme, la mort l'est
contre une orée qui bruit, qui chatoie, vaine à mesure.

Tu ne demeures pas précipitée dans ce trou,
sibylle consultante,
si le temps, si l'espace, ton grand corps les déborde,
répandu hors d'accès,
laissant passer par l'indistincte bouche,
dans l'aridité monotone du paroxysme,
d'intermittents grommellements,
échos des diverses profondeurs.

Tu cries ce qui te vient, tu ignorais le savoir,
prophétesse, aussitôt tu le perds.
Tu le répètes, qui surgis...Tu l'oublies. Tu
n'oublies pas.

Rumeurs de l'inacceptable... Rumeurs
de l'inaccompli.
Femme géante vierge et porteuse de lait.
Réfractaire. Inentendue.

...Death is not silent in this hateful voice,
where it does not dream and curse alone.
If life is a claim against its term, death is one
against a margin that rumbles, shimmers, just as vain.

You do not stay long plunged into that hole,
conferring sibyl,
if time, if space, your great body exceeds them,
spreading out of reach,
letting slip through your obscure mouth,
in the monotonous dryness of paroxysm,
intermittent mutterings,
echoes of the various depths.

You cry what comes to you, unaware of knowing it,
prophetess, straight away you lose it.
You repeat it as you emerge...You forget it. You
do not forget.

Rumblings of the unacceptable... Rumblings
of the unfinished.
Virgin giantess, bearer of milk.
Refractory. Unheard.

[V]

Celui qui ouvre et qui ferme les portes
aux désirs furieux, dénie, attise, Janus,
le monstre honnête à porter double face,
a-t-il aussi destin de présider
au transport accompli de l'une à l'autre aurore?

– On dit qu'aucune forme n'a été prescrite
pour le sacrifice, que nul ne sait
quelles offrandes seront reçues, qu'il suffirait
que tous aillent en quête, que la récrimination
cessât, que le défi, la rage,
se changent en élan, invocation, confiance.
– Il ne s'agit que de donner tout et d'être prêt.
– Il ne faudrait que retenir son souffle.

...Qui a prononcé l'événement? Si nul
n'a parlé, chacun dans son cœur a entendu
quand il a lu les signes...La jeune fille
a vu l'ange, aussitôt elle a su
que le poids incertain de l'an qui va finir,
l'avorté, le manquant, grossi au flanc des âges,
tout allait s'accomplir et se confondre en joie.

– Tout le poids dans son ventre, l'innocente a dit oui.

– La fille de l'homme...

– Ô pieuse vierge, délice des roseaux!

– La mère de l'homme...

Le sang des témoins approuvait les témoins.
Sur l'étagement pétré des nuages quelqu'un monte,
c'est Dieu même, il se tourne vers nous, il confirme:
Souris à ta mère, mon enfant radieux...

[V]

He who opens and closes the doors
on wild desires, denies, stirs up, Janus,
the monster decently two-faced,
is he destined to preside
over delight achieved from one to the other dawn?

– It is said that no form has been prescribed
for sacrifice, that no one knows
which offerings will be received, that it would suffice
that everyone should go in search, that recrimination
should cease, that challenge, rage,
should change to uplift, invocation, trust.
– Just give your all and be prepared.
– You have only to hold your breath.

...Who said what was to happen? Even if no one
spoke, each one in his heart understood
when he read the signs...The girl
saw the angel, straight away she knew
that the uncertain weight of the dying year,
miscarried, missing, great in the womb of time,
was all to be fulfilled, to melt in joy.

– With all the weight in her belly, the innocent said yes.

– The daughter of man...

– O pious maid, delight of reeds!

– The mother of man...

The blood of the witnesses sanctioned the witnesses.
Someone is climbing the stony terrace of the clouds,
it is God himself, he is turning towards us, confirming:
Smile at your mother, my radiant child...

– Se voyaient-ils,
quand ils se regardaient au profond des yeux,
le grand garçon et la jeune femme?

Quand deux envols d'oiseaux de part en part
se sont mêlés,
s'enfonce l'azur, indéfiniment s'exalte
l'empire de la mer.

...Est-ce lui le premier qui a rougi
devant une forme qui changeait, se chargeait,
l'énorme corps dressé...aussitôt s'affaissa.

L'année s'assombrit encore, qui touche au terme.
Dans le défilé qui s'étrécit, quelle soudaine
avidité de retourner jusqu'en la voûte ancienne.
...La nuit trop pleine a crevé son sac,
et s'éparpillent les serpents des derniers jours.
Tout se réduit, se consterne. Comment
conjurer, ralentir si le malheur
devait se retrouver?
Fatale est l'année et descend encore... Espoir?

Quand se retourne le sablier,
par l'étroite fente de la nuit la plus longue,
un nouvel an naïf déjà remue un œil...
À pas de plus en plus larges, le jeune soleil
a entamé sa route – c'est la même.
Et la redoutable ramène ses cuisses géantes.
Elle a pris une autre dégaine: de vieille,
le visage éclairé d'un sourire très doux.

– Did they see themselves,
when they gazed deep into each other's eyes,
the tall fellow and the young woman?

When two flocks of birds mingle
with one another,
the sky's blue deepens, the empire of the sea
is magnified indefinitely.

...Was he the first to blush
before a shape that was changing, gaining weight,
its huge body upright... straight away collapsed.

The year darkens further, which touches its end.
In the narrowing pass, what sudden
eagerness to return even to the ancient vault.
...Night, overfull, has burst its bag,
and the snakes of the last days are dispersing.
Everything shrinks, dismayed. How
ward off, slow down, if trouble
were to return?
Fatal, the year continues down...What of hope?

When the hourglass is reversed,
through the narrow slit of the longest night,
a callow new year already blinks an eye...
With ever longer strides, the young sun
has set out on its way – the same way.
And the fearsome one revives her giant thighs.
She is walking differently: like an old woman,
her face aglow now with the sweetest smile.

[VI]

Ils sont en famille, ils vont en bande. Faisaient la fête.
Par un grand matin partis, avec un ours et un âne,
sur des chemins qui n'avançaient pas,
ils les ont laissés avec l'encens, la myrrhe...
Les motocyclettes bronchent et pétaradent.
Illuminés aux milles flammes des lieux saints,
ils descendent le grand escalier. Attendus
par le souvenir d'un enfant, est-ce qu'ils l'adorent?

Remuent-ils des lèvres pour expliquer ou comprendre
les gestes des statues entre les baraques foraines?
C'est la nuit et le grand jour, et soleil la neige.
Dans la rue qui regorge, les emblèmes dressés.
Par le tumulte des pas, les girandoles,
un silence intimidé se glisse.
Au plus noir du minuit, n'en finit pas
la montée étincelante, l'œuf.

Il y a les trois églises, les larges draperies rouges.
Le berceau, la table chatoient.
Ruelles qui tournent, rangées muettes, parois lourdes.
Les cloches sans répit. Des glissements d'eau vive.
Il y avait des grottes, des colonnes, la barrière.
Et la source brûlante avec des chevaux morts,
par morceaux blancs comme des nouveau-nés
jetés dans l'eau entre les buis, des touffes de crinière.

Oh! pénétrer dans la fontaine quand elle bouillonnera,
comme autrefois souriante,
pour en sortir avec le manteau du vainqueur...
Ils ont attendu cette nuit en tremblant, tous se précipitent.
Mais oseront-ils?

74

[VI]

A family, out together. Making merry.
Early one morning, with a bear and an ass,
along roads heading nowhere,
they let them loose with incense, myrrh...
Motorcycles lurch, backfire.
Lit with the thousand flames of holy places,
they descend the great stairs. Waited upon
by the memory of a child, do they adore it?

Do their lips move to explain or understand
the gestures of statues between travelling booths?
It is night and broad daylight, sunlit snow.
In the packed street, the emblems are set up.
Through the din of footsteps, the girandoles,
a cowed silence slips in.
The darkest midnight brings no end
to the sparkling upshoot, the egg.

There are the three churches, the wide red draperies.
The cradle, the table shimmer.
Winding alleys, dumb rows, heavy walls.
The bells relentless. Living water sliding.
There used to be caves, columns, the turnpike.
And the burning spring with dead horses,
with scattered tufts of mane white as newborn babies
flung in the water between scraps of boxwood.

Oh! to step into the pool when it is troubled,
as once it did smiling,
to emerge with the robe of conqueror...
They have waited trembling for this night, they all rush forward.
But will they dare?

On avait dit aussi qu'il faut prendre garde
à ne pas fixer le regard des loups
qui déambulent par la foule, ces jours-là,
ou qui se tiennent dans les maisons pavoisées
tout alentour de la place ronde,
immobiles à certaines fenêtres et penchés,
habillés pareil aux autres. Un rien
d'un peu triangulaire dans le visage
ne suffit pas à les dénoncer.
L'un ou l'autre peut s'y tromper, qui ne se trompe
cette nuit-là,
si la fête bat son plein sous déguisement?

Oh! pénétrer dans la fontaine quand elle bouillonnera
comme autrefois souriante,
pour en sortir avec le manteau du vainqueur...
– Elle attendra cette nuit en tremblant
toute la vie, mais oseront-ils?

– Et la vieille a fini sa tournée dans la nuit.
Son profil variable s'est doré pour chacun
tout un instant sur le seuil obscur
quand elle procédait, maison après maison,
à la distribution des friandises...
Déjà lointaine l'aurore, quand les enfants
découvrent qu'ils attendaient la vraie source de joie.
Et les éboueurs, sur les dents, ramassent
les vaisselles jetées – brisées pendant le festin.
Chaque année ils en font une nouvelle colline
avec au sommet, statue de leur saint patron.
Et les Sept, les antiques et très glorieuses,
par les aboiements feutrés de la lune
grognent et se redressent
comme les tétines d'une louve ou d'une truie.

It had been said too that we must beware
of catching the eye of wolves
as they slink among the crowd on those days,
or lurk in the houses decked with bunting
all about the round piazza,
motionless at certain windows and leaning out, ·
dressed like the rest. Something
vaguely three-cornered about the face
is not enough to expose them.
Anyone can be mistaken, who is not
on that night,
if the feast is in full swing though in disguise?

Oh! to step into the pool when it is troubled,
as once it did smiling,
to emerge with the robe of conqueror...
– It will wait trembling for this night
all its life, but will they dare?

– And the old woman has done her night patrol.
Her shifting shape glows gold for everyone
a whole moment on the dim threshold
when, house by house, she went about her business
dishing out dainties...
Dawn is already far away when children
learn that they were expecting the real source of joy.
And the road-sweepers, knackered, gather
crockery thrown out – broken during the banquet.
Each year they heap it into a new hill
topped with a statue of their patron saint.
And the Seven Hills, ancient and most glorious,
while the moon bays in muted tones,
grumble and re-form upright
like the dugs of a she-wolf or a sow.

[VII]

Déjà s'affermissait dans l'affrontement
l'éclat puissant et noir. La peur
s'enfonçant dans la nuit pour composer
des représentations aventureuses,
hachurait les années enfantines.

Qui sait prévenir et subvenir? Qui interdit?
Qui ordonne et châtie? Qui distribue les charges?
Qui donnera le pouvoir – qui atermoie?

Je me soulèverai à l'extrême d'un désir
dont j'ignore l'effigie. De degré en degré,
appliqué à tout ordonner, je gravis, j'accède.

Exposé sur le fleuve aurait été moins sombre,
m'éloignant de la rive...

J'avancerai à la rencontre de tous ennemis,
sous la cuirasse où se dérobe l'offense.
On ne saurait s'égarer à défendre la patrie.
Je prends appui à la terre, je m'agrippe à mes pas.
De la légion de bêtes qui gonflent ma poitrine,
je me formerai troupe en ordre. Je me conformerai
à la Loi, je me confirmerai à la servir. J'obéis,
à mon tour j'exerce le commandement.

[VII]

Already the powerful black flash
was hardening in defiance. Fear
burrowing in the darkness to devise
adventurous performances,
was carving lines across the years of childhood.

Who knows to warn and help out? Who forbids?
Who orders and chastises? Who appoints?
Who will empower – who grants a stay?

I will arise at the limit of a desire
whose likeness I do not know. Step by step,
ready to order all things, I climb, comply.

Abandoned on the river would have been less dismal,
moving away from the bank...

I will go forward to face all enemies,
beneath the breastplate that conceals the offence.
You could not go far wrong defending the fatherland.
I take support from the ground, I plant my feet.
From the legion of beasts that swell my bosom,
I will form up my troop. I will conform
to the Law, confirm myself in its service. I obey,
in turn I exercise command.

...Les premières alarmes dans les taillis querelleurs,
le culte des dieux lares et le respect filial,
la lecture des entrailles et l'envol
du côté favorable, les souillures
et les sacrifices, l'initiation, les quolibets,
les dissensions vaincues, le dévoilement
du projet des conjurés, les nouveaux troubles
et la riposte aux confins, l'établissement
de remparts avancés et la réduction à l'unité.

Et la grande courbure de l'univers,
reprise en gloire au pourtour du Colosseo,
les clameurs qui proclament, en cercles s'immensifiant,
totalité conquise... Et regarde, tout est vide.
Une enfant pâle et qui saigne
entre les blocs renversés, le serpent
parmi les touffes du laurier sauvage.
Et les hanches sans respect d'une femme ébauchée,
énorme, étendue...

De nouveau les palais qui s'entassent, les arcs dressés.
Des aqueducs intègres par la campagne
et les entrées solennelles de l'eau dans la ville.
La foule sur les escaliers, qui s'acclamait.

...Hauts frontons, colonnes, colonnades, trophées,
grottes fendues et fissure ouvragée,
bouche tendue, pierre tranchée, entablement,
globe affronté, verge embrasée, brandissement.
Muscles roulant, rangées meurtries, corps exhaussés!
Labyrinthe enfoncé, largesses par les rues.
Déferlement de cloches, les eaux à la volée!

– *Ma!* Trop d'orgueil.

...The first alarms in the feuding thickets,
worship of household gods, filial piety,
reading of entrails, flight of birds
in the auspicious direction, stains
and sacrifices, initiation, gibes,
opposition overcome, disclosure
of conspiracy, new troubles
and border counter-attack, erection
of forward bulwarks and reduction to one unit.

And the great curvature of the universe,
gloriously matched in the sweep of the Colosseum,
the clamour that proclaims, building up in circles,
the whole world conquered... And look, it is all empty.
A pale girl bleeding
between the upturned blocks, the serpent
amid the clumps of wild laurel.
And the wanton hips of a woman in outline,
enormous, stretched out...

Again the palaces piling up, the arches raised.
Honest aqueducts throughout the countryside
and the solemn watergates of the city.
The crowd on stairways cheering.

...Tall pediments, columns, colonnades, trophies,
caves cleft and each cleft carved,
a mouth pursed, a stone hewn, a tablet,
a level orb, a rod recessed, arms brandished.
Muscles rippling, bruised rows, uplifted bodies!
A sunken labyrinth, bounty in the streets.
Bells unfurling, waters flying about!

– *Ma!* Too much pride.

Titan fragile, géant ornementé.
Foudre, torrent, massue, musculature vaine,
travestis de la gloire, déesses inventées,
sur les trop hautes marches, Hercule faux miroir,
solitude fardée, redoublements vantards,
phrases et emphase du marbre en marche,
étalement de mille silhouettes et trompettes,
à la fin tagliatelle gesticulant!

Frail Titan, ornamented giant.
Thunderbolt, torrent, bludgeon, useless brawn,
a travesty of glory, invented goddesses,
on steps too high, Hercules a false mirror,
painted solitude, boastful redoublings,
sentences, emphases of marble in motion,
displays of a thousand silhouettes and trumpets,
so many noodles waving!

VIII

Le suprême Jupiter, le Redentore,
qui nous a donné la Loi avec le salut,
meurt-il à chaque monument qui l'érige?
Ou bien s'il dort, s'il est emporté par la foule,
engourdi dans leurs cœurs sans qu'ils y prennent garde,
pour se réveiller à minuit dans chaque maison,
dans son petit nid originel, vipérin,
très chaud et très bon, ici et partout au monde?

– Nous demeurons dans nos maisons, dans nos familles,
Nous récitons nos prières au pied du lit.
Nous honorons nos lares. À écouter nos cœurs,
nous n'y entendons pas malice. Nos enfants
nous ressemblent et c'est un grand plaisir.
C'est notre dévotion la plus tendre,
Gesú Bambino, Madonna Mamma, Papà.

Le pape est sous son dôme, et sa calotte blanche.
Tiare à la main, le pied traînant, pleure avec tous.
Ses acolytes régneront-ils? Bouches des anges
à jamais closes, leur pouvoir se fait petit.

Si la lumière, au soir tombant, se laisse choir
par habitude, en anciens lambeaux d'or,
l'encens s'évanouit des lieux saints aujourd'hui,
comme s'est dissipée plus avant
l'odeur épaisse des bêtes sacrifiées.
Les pas des âges effacent
les traits des seigneurs sur les dalles funéraires.

– Vieil homme qui se tient en retrait,
il s'étonne de sourire avec majesté.
Les fils ont pour lui de la compassion.

VIII

Does supreme Jupiter, the Redentore,
who gave us the Law and salvation with it,
die every time a monument exalts him?
Or if he sleeps, if he is borne off by the crowd,
numb in their hearts without their noticing,
to wake at midnight in every house,
in his little primal nest, of vipers,
very snug, very cosy, here and everywhere else?

– We stay in our homes, with our families.
We say our prayers at the foot of the bed.
We honour our household gods. Listening to our hearts,
we hear no illwill. Our children
look like us and that is a great pleasure.
This is our tenderest devotion,
Gesú Bambino, Madonna Mamma, Papà.

The pope is beneath his dome, and his white skull-cap.
Tiara in hand, foot dragging, weeps with all.
Will his acolytes reign? Mouths of angels
for ever closed, their power is growing less.

If light at eventide lets itself fall
from habit in its former shreds of gold,
the incense fades today from holy places,
as earlier the thick smell
of sacrificial beasts dwindled away.
The footsteps of the ages wear away
features of lords on their memorial slabs.

– An old man who keeps in the background,
he is surprised to smile majestically.
The sons feel compassion for him.

– Le corps divin a fondu sans y mettre jouissance
aujourd'hui. Ne lui avais-tu pas donné ton sein,
Grande Mère de l'agonie de Dieu?

– Corps en péril, je touche
le corps du saint avec amour. J'entre à ta main
dans le verger. Je t'institue
ma protectrice, vierge, par droit d'amour.

...Nous allons en cortège, nous entonnons ensemble
l'alleluia à la source de vie.
Nous avançons chez nous dans la maison du père,
y goûtons le pain délicieux.
Dans les voix qui se répondent, se retrouvent,
nous reconnaissons la voix perdue,
nous recouvrons notre parole.

– Gémissez, multitude amère de Rome.

Filles, emportant à vos seins qui sourdent
l'innombrable innocent.
Gémissez, femmes aux lèvres taries,
car le vrai père ne se cache pas non plus
dans l'hostie resplendissante.
Et la vierge, sur le pavement oublié,
frissonne en vain
entre les bras dressés du Gesú.

Ô Michelangelo da Caravaggio,
trattoria pourpre des nourritures,
où les anges sont des nôtres, les chevaux attentifs,
étends les bras pour prendre, abreuve-nous ici,
sur la croix entrouverte de genoux qui s'écartent
et d'un corps qui se hausse!

– The divine body has melted without giving pleasure
today. Had you not given him your breast,
Great Mother of God's agony?

– A body in peril, I touch
the saint's body with love. At your hand
I enter the orchard. I appoint you
my protector, virgin, by right of love.

...We walk in procession, we intone together
the alleluia to the source of life.
We go on homeward into our father's house,
taste there the delicious bread.
In the voices that answer, rediscover each other,
we recognise the lost voice,
we recover our speech.

– Groan, bitter multitude of Rome.

Girls, bearing off at your welling breasts
the countless innocent.
Groan, women with parched lips,
for the true father is not hidden either
in the glittering Host.
And the virgin, on the forgotten pavement,
trembles in vain
in the raised arms of the Gesú.

O Michelangelo da Caravaggio,
purple trattoria of sustenance,
where the angels are ours, the horses attentive,
stretch out your arms to take, refresh us here,
upon the gaping cross of parted knees
and of a body reaching up!

La croix se formera de deux bouleaux tremblants,
se touchent en leur milieu, les limites en flammes,
une félicité terrible les emporte.

... Lentes rangées, coquille ourlée, rumeur veinée,
sourde fontaine fauve, minotaure qui va,
et le vaisseau des larmes, la chasseresse en armes,
dépassés poursuivant, l'un par l'autre aboli,
naissance, à l'infini, mille mêlées du feu.

Le même s'est défait en deux morceaux fuyards,

innombrables remous depuis toujours en quête.

Et la Vierge, rencontrant Messaline,
la vulve insomnieuse,
la baisa sur le front et la bénit.
Et il se fit des désordres dans les parages,
et d'autres dieux, à pas de loup se sont glissés
sous les tables des Lois et dans les gorges, puis
ils ont chu.
Car nul ne règne. Pas la joie,
ni l'innocence, ni le plaisir, ni la vertu.
Sous un autre visage le héros recommence,
naïf, ses hauts faits. Il tombe.

The cross will be formed of two quivering birch trees,
they touch in the middle, outer limbs aflame,
borne off by a terrible bliss.

...Slow rows, a trimmed shell, a veined rumble,
a dull wild fountain, a walking minotaur,
and the vessel of tears, the armed huntress,
all gone past in pursuit, cancelling each other,
birth without end, a thousand clashes of fire.

The same has split in two runaway pieces,

unnumbered eddies ever since in search.

And the Virgin, meeting Messalina,
the unsleeping vulva,
kissed her upon the brow and blessed her.
And there was unrest in the outlying parts,
and other gods slipped stealthily beneath
the tables of the Laws, down throats, and then
they fell.
For none reigns. Not joy,
nor innocence, nor pleasure, nor virtue.
In other guise the hero naively
begins again his mighty deeds. He drops.

En vain les blessés multiplient les offrandes,
les confesseurs et les démagogues,
intercesseurs à toutes bannières,
prononcent la parole, et le peuple acquiesce.
En vain ils affluent, ils saluent, ils écument,
déferlent en vivat,
ils forment en rond l'ardent simulacre.
Pêle-mêle on emporte, sang dans la sciure,
le corps virginal tronçonné,
les lions vaincus par le miracle.
Nul cérémonial, fût-ce avec trépignements,
couronne ou serpents d'or, immolation,
ne saura combler
la même impatience par tout l'être dispersé.

Et les voiles des vierges et les attributs des saints,
en plein marbre fauve, se soulèvent et se dressent
pour le millénaire témoignage.
L'ange musclé se rue sur la trompette et proclame
baliverne de gloire.
L'Immacolata règne sur les serpents.

In vain the wounded pile on offerings,
confessors, demagogues,
intercessors of every hue,
make utterances, and the people yield.
In vain they flock, they hail, they foam,
break out into hurrahs,
they gather round in a show of eagerness.
In confusion, with blood among the scraps,
the lopped virgin body,
the lions conquered by miracle are borne off.
No ceremonial, even with stamping feet,
no crown or golden serpents, no immolation,
can ever satisfy
the same impatience throughout the scattered being.

And the virgins' veils and the saints' attributes,
in full lurid marble, rise up and take their place
for the testimony of a thousand years.
The muscular angel rushes to the trumpet and proclaims
glorious twaddle.
The Immacolata reigns over the serpents.

Aux grands hommes, si la patrie reconnaît
statue géante, c'est plus tard,
et la pierre veinée n'accorde nul bonheur sanguin.
Au rythme des jeunes cœurs, tâtonnante,
la renommée prendra sa voix
quand le défunt aura donné
au myrthe noir son éclat pâle.

– Et une fois déjà son souvenir
avait rendu espoir au peuple… Et s'il a causé
du trouble dans un cœur, tel autre découvrira
fierté à cause de lui. Toutes sortes de larmes.
Désir de surpasser, sacrifices, vertige… Verbiage!
Amour de soi, oubli du mort, les honneurs déplorables.
Et toute cette barbe en marbre, bien ourlée,
ne pousse pas sur ses joues plus qu'aux statues des dieux!

Tombeaux parés, les berceaux trop confiants.
Pourquoi les disposer, les accès précieux?
Qui poursuit sa vie là, qui peut y découvrir
l'Amour ici-bas pressenti?

Ni le blé qui sait renaître, ni le grand arbre
que les entrailles de la Terre-Mère font reverdir,
ni le sang du taureau, ni la semence du martyr,
nulle promesse, pour nous, ne sera tenue.

– Seulement une fois…
Un enfant précautionneux dans le malheur,
le même qui criait dans la chambre du haut,
sorti des lourdes paumes de la géante,
et jusqu'au moment d'être repris au magma,
qui va portant son vieux cartable,
et qui tressaute si lui revient
cette étrangère voix familière.

[IX]

To great men, if the fatherland honours them
with a giant statue, it is too late,
and the veined stone grants no full-blooded happiness.
From the rhythm of young hearts, fumbling
fame will take its voice
when the dead man has given
his pale lustre to black myrtle.

– And once already his memory
had restored hope to the people... And if he has brought
trouble to a heart, someone else will discover
pride on account of him. All sorts of tears.
An urge to surpass, to sacrifice, to swoon... Drivel!
Self-love, disregard of the dead, lamentable honours.
And all that marble beard, well trimmed,
glows on its cheeks no more than on the statues of gods!

Decked tombs, the cradles too trusting.
Why set them out, the precious approaches?
Who lives his life there, who can discover
Love foreshadowed here below?

Neither the corn that knows rebirth, nor the great tree
made green again by the guts of Mother Earth,
nor the bull's blood, nor the martyr's seed,
no promise, for us, will be kept.

– Only once...
A child wary in wretchedness,
the same who called out from the upper room,
emerging from the giantess's heavy palms,
and till the moment he was swallowed in the magma,
which sweeps along his old satchel,
and judders if that foreign
familiar voice returns.

Oh! Dans le tombeau tremblant, la source.
La seule félicité de la vie, frères!
Si elle te ravit sur tes chemins, t'inonde,
tu ne sauras te reconnaître plus qu'un instant
dans les grandes eaux sans mémoire.
Ne l'attends pas, cette grâce hagarde...
L'ancienne. Le retour à la patrie désirable.
Où t'entraînerait-elle, cette bouche muette?
Pas à pas, sans répit, ta vie s'enfonce.
Elle se ravale dans le même battement,
l'énergie récidiviste... Pas au-delà,
pas au-delà d'une dernière oscillation.

– Nous passons dans les rues, nous allons notre vie
dans l'animation des mouvements au soleil.
On est à son affaire, on y croit presque,
certains jours, s'il fait beau.

... Au-dessous, ce n'est pas la mort déjà,
plutôt des caravansérails très actifs,
qu'organisent dans leur angoisse et dans leur rage
les figures échappées de toi, captives
qui te gouvernent. Il y a
des étranglements. Comme des bêtes,
qui se déplacent à toutes profondeurs.
Mille flèches pour fondre
sur toi d'en bas. Des mains
pour t'interdire ou te précipiter.
Ou peut-être n'y a-t-il qu'un arbre, immense
réseau de sève et de blessures. Une terre meuble,
qui respire et bruit dans la ténèbre. Rien
que ton souffle. Des sanglots. Parfois
quelque chose en sort, bat des ailes.

Oh! In the trembling tomb, the spring.
Life's only bliss, brothers! If it
snatches you on the road, overwhelms you,
you will not know yourself for more than an instant
in the great forgetful waters.
Don't wait for that frantic grace...
Of old. Going back to the fair fatherland.
Where would it draw you, that unspeaking mouth?
Step by step, relentless, your life sinks.
It drags itself down in the same beat,
the energy that knows no better... A step beyond,
not beyond one last swing.

– We pass into the streets, we go our life
as quickened by the motions in the sun.
We are at business, almost think we are,
on certain days, if it is fine.

...Below, it is not death already,
rather some bustling caravanserais,
organised in their anguish and their rage
fugitive forms of you, captives
that govern you. There are
tight spots. Like beasts
shifting about at all depths.
A thousand arrows to pounce
upon you from below. Hands
to bar your way or urge you on.
Or perhaps there is only a tree, a huge
network of sap and wounds. A mobile earth
breathing and sounding in the dark. Nothing
but your breath. Some sobs. Sometimes
something comes out, flaps wings.

[X]

Montagne de tessons et de trognons,
Testaccio, chef et corps stériles, pyramide
qui ne sait pas frémir.
Mais la vie qui s'est perdue innombrablement,
notre vie qui s'enfonce, qui perdure, est retenue.
Comme ses grandes pelletées immobilisées
tout à coup remuent.

Il y eut
ces premières glissées par les verdures,
et sous le fouet de l'orage luxuriant
se découvrirent les seins de la fillette nubile.
Plus tard,
dans le renfoncement, sous l'ouverture haute,
un archipel d'odeurs s'élève du creux des corps,
et la mer est là, sauvage et l'origine...
Ornée de seins précieux, rousse, le chien en laisse,
attentive, la signora débouche sous les portiques.
Ô matrone creuse! Et mamma grosse! La maison vaine!
Et les nouvelles amours qui s'aigrissent:
les rondes fesses, le dernier remploi du désir poursuivant,
l'enfance toujours là, l'incorrigible.

– Millions de pas à la sortie des bureaux.
Rapides riens à la Cafeteria. L'on repart.
Les tramways qui s'empoignent. Le parcours ferraillant. Le bel été.
Les rencontres, les blagues, les agaceries.
Puis l'approche hésitante des corps, la suffocation éblouie,
les grandes lanières du désir, le lent supplice de la vie,
les gémissements dans la maison du faubourg,
l'allée d'ifs noirs, le cercueil en allé,
le repas sur les cendres avec les parents,
l'ultime fiasque vidée.

[X]

A mountain of potsherds and stumps,
Testaccio, head and body barren, a pyramid
unshakeable.
But life that has been wasted times without number,
our life that sinks, that endures, is hung on to.
As its great stilled spadefuls
suddenly stir.

There were
those first slidings through the greenery,
and beneath the lash of the luxuriant storm
the breasts of the nubile girl were then revealed.
Later,
down in the hollow, below the high opening,
the body secretes an archipelago of smells,
and the sea is there, wild and the origin...
Adorned with precious breasts, a redhead, her dog on a lead,
the signora, attentive, steps out beneath the porches.
O roomy matron! And fat mamma! The vain house!
And the new loves going sour:
round buttocks, desire the pursuer used one last time,
childhood still there, beyond reproof.

– Millions of footsteps as the offices close.
Brief babble in the Cafeteria. Then homeward.
Trams being grabbed. The homeward grind. The fine summer.
Meetings, jokes, flirtations.
Then the hesitant approach of bodies, the dazzled gasp,
the great thongs of desire, the slow torture of life,
the groans in the suburban house,
the path between black yews, the coffin departed,
the meal on ashes with relatives,
the final flask drained.

Dans les carrières habitées par les morts,
les dieux avec les hommes se sont parlé autrefois,
penchés les uns vers les autres pour se protéger.
Mais des dieux plus anciens dans l'homme
sont là qui veillent. Des bêtes qui rampent
se lèvent, la voix rompue.
Les prodigues, les renégats, les fuyards qui s'entravent.
La rivalité qui recommence avec d'autres.
Fureur mal ravalée, messagers lapidés,
vieillards achevés quand ils se rendent, agneaux
cloués aux portes, le gouffre, en ses vapeurs
très fécond.

– Glorieux, le soleil
s'est ocré au flanc des murs géants.
Dans les marchés des quartiers, l'azur doré chemine
avec bonhomie entre l'aubergine et les citrons.
Dans la rue où l'on forge, dans celle où l'on ravaude
les tapisseries déchirées de la nuit,
dans la rue où les antiques Mères nous initient,
sur la place où se concertaient un millier d'hirondelles,
dans la rue des prêtres froids et des étuves,
des bains sur le fleuve enlisé.

– D'un cirque qui fut, l'ovale d'une prairie demeure,
sommé de tours délabrées, proclamant
la nostalgie du pouvoir souverain
quand les pauvres changent de mouvance.
Des chiens féroces lâchés, les fauteurs qui hésitent,
la conciliation rusée, les représailles
remises à plus tard, les faucheurs
de long en large près de la mer.

In the quarries inhabited by the dead,
gods and men spoke together long ago,
leaning towards each other for protection.
But more ancient gods in man
are there and watching. Crawling beasts
rise up, their voices cracked.
Prodigals, renegades, fugitives jammed together.
Rivalries renewed.
Fury still foaming, messengers stoned,
old men done for when they give up, lambs
nailed to doors, the abyss, in its fumes
most fruitful.

– Glorious, the sun
has turned ochre on the side of giant walls.
In the local markets, the gilded blue cheerfully
ambles between aubergine and lemons.
In the street of smiths, in the one where they stitch up
the torn tapestries of the night,
in the street where the old Mothers put us in the know,
in the square where a thousand swallows used to twitter,
in the street of the cold priests and the bath-houses,
baths on the sunken river.

– Of a circus that was, an oval of meadowland remains,
topped with dilapidated towers, proclaiming
nostalgia for sovereign power
when the poor change fiefdom.
Fierce dogs running loose, the abettors hesitant,
wily conciliation, reprisals
put off till later, the reapers
to and fro near the sea.

Dans les nuages qui font arrêt au-dessus de nous,
lisibles noirs,
venus des parages des collines,
des *fattorie* apparaissent, pauvres et auprès
des maisons de paille, découpées comme des viandes,
pour le manger des bêtes et la litière.
Une ruine d'aqueduc passe en geignant.
Solennel, un concile de rochers, au soir tombant,
endormie la terre alentour,
puis le glissement rouge de la lumière.

... ET LA GRISERIE DORÉE DES LOINTAINES ÉTABLES,
ET LES PAUVRES, CONFINÉS DANS LES PRÉS MAIGRES,
APPARURENT PAR LA BRUME, ILLUMINÉS SUR LES FAÇADES
LES PLUS HAUTES, À CE DÉFAUT DU JOUR.

... Et les motocyclettes et les combines
de ceux qui les montent, la chaleur claironnant
à la Saint-Jean-d'Été, le goudron qui empoisse
tout ce fin bas violet, la rumeur
de la grande canicule à travers les persiennes,
hors d'usage, ces deux corps mâles, suant, suffoqués.

Et les épluchures pourrissent sur les dalles.
Les graffiti bronzés, signatures anonymes
tracées à la sauvette dans les encoignures
pour le soulagement du bas-ventre,
par la solitude énorme, dimanche, été,
marquent aussi bien tes couleurs, homme,
que le marbre.

Et de la stature des lions affrontés,
la patte gélive mordue par trop d'hivers
s'effrite et le blason chancelle.
Et le vin roule au Trastevere
dans les caveaux souterrains,
les sentences des buveurs prennent place
dans la sagesse éternelle de la Ville.

100

In the clouds stacking above us,
legibly black,
come from the hilly parts,
fattorie appear, poor and beside
houses of straw, cut up like meat,
for fodder and litter.
A ruined aqueduct goes by whimpering.
Solemn, a council of rocks, at eventide,
the land around asleep,
then the red sliding of the night.

...AND THE GILDED EUPHORIA OF DISTANT STABLES,
AND THE POOR, CONFINED IN THE LEAN MEADOWS,
APPEARED THROUGH THE MIST, LIT UP AGAINST THE TALLEST
HOUSE-FRONTS, AS THIS DAY WAS FADING.

...And the motorcycles and the schemes
of the riders, the heat trumpeting
to St John of Midsummer, the tar that coats
all that fine purple stocking, the rumble
of the great dog-day heard through the slatted blinds,
unwonted, those two male bodies, sweating, gasping.

And the refuse rots upon the flagstones.
The bronzed graffiti, anonymous signatures
scratched in corners during a quick exit
to ease the bowel,
hugely alone, on Sunday, in summer,
mark out your colours just as well, man,
as marble can.

And from the stature of the affronted lions,
the paw frostbitten by too many winters
crumbles and the escutcheon totters.
And the wine ripples to Trastevere
into the underground vaults,
the judgements of drinkers take their place
in the eternal wisdom of the City.

...Et les motocyclistes et les trombines
de ceux qui les montent, la chaleur s'engouffrant
par l'escalier défait, le goudron qui empoisse
les couvertures jaunes, le grondement
de la voix ancienne à travers les persiennes.

Dans l'enfilade des hauts greniers du palais,
l'adolescent forcé s'abandonne aux vicaires à la fin
et jouit.

...And the bikers and the mugs
of those who ride them, the heat engulfed
down the broken stair, the tar that coats
the yellow coverings, the snarl
of the ancient voice heard through the slatted blinds.
Passing through the palace's high garrets,
youth under pressure gives in finally to the priests
and has fun.

[XI]

Les pieds dans la flaque sale,
toute la bande avec les filles pareilles,
près des gazomètres de la via Appia Antica,
où l'on élève des lapins dans de nobles tombeaux
– ils rêvassent, ils ressassent, faisaient les braves,
les enfants sans aveu.
Des bruits lourds dans le ciel passent, qu'ils regardent.

... L'odeur de la futaille au soleil rouge,
le charroi dans les feuilles mortes, les peupliers tranchés,
des paysannes puissantes, nues,
dans les grandes salles apportant les plats,
les tanks et les flammes qui s'avancent
parmi le blé versé, la montée
des eaux limoneuses emportant les soldats,
la Mère qui appelle et qui les frappe,
la traversée, l'aboiement noir...

Et l'énorme figure s'est trouvée au milieu d'eux,
tout à coup sur la place close – depuis toujours là.
Mais qui saurait la voir? Qui saurait reconnaître,
saisi par l'imperceptible, par l'inexorable frémissement,
les deux faces
d'un seul grand corps qui s'enfle, englobe tout,
s'évanouit,
et qui se dresse double encore en le combat
– amples cuisses, rictus affronté, les dents –
qui t'annule, qui s'allongeait, qui naît...

Qui s'acharnait?
Qui poursuit sa naissance? Qui supporte les plaies?
Qui voulait usurper, mais qui abdiquera?
Qui demandait pardon? Qui pouvait l'accorder?
Qui a machiné notre Loi? Qui
inventera l'innocence?

[XI]

Their feet in the dirty puddle,
the whole band with identical girls,
near the gas-holders of the via Appia Antica,
where rabbits are raised in noble tombs
– they muse, they ruminate, used to brag,
vagrant children.
Heavy noises in the sky pass, which they watch.

...The smell of the cask in the red sunlight,
the transport in the dead leaves, the poplars chopped up,
powerful, naked peasant women
in the great halls bringing dishes,
the tanks and the flames advancing
among the laid corn, the rise
of muddy waters bearing the soldiers off,
the Mother calling and striking them,
the crossing, the black barking...

And the huge figure was there in their midst,
suddenly in the closed square – had always been there.
But who might see it? Who might recognise,
seized by the imperceptible, by the inexorable shudder,
the two aspects
of one great body swelling, including all,
vanishing,
and rearing double still in the fight
– ample thighs, unflinching grin, teeth –
wiping you out, grown longer, being born...

Who was hounding?
Who pursues his birth? Who bears the wounds?
Who would usurp, but who will abdicate?
Who sought forgiveness? Who could grant it then?
Who has contrived our Law? Who
will invent innocence?

[XII]

Je fuis sous les huées,
par les arrières de la colline où portant la couronne,
ils préparent le triomphe. J'entends les tambours
voilés qui battent, et les marches gravies.
La haute fontaine vole en éclats. Des chiens immobiles
devant chaque porche tout au long des arcades,
les babines retroussées...
Mêlé aux arrivants dont la troupe s'allonge,
se disperse, j'avance entraîné par la voix,
je tourne, encore on tourne, on débouche sur la place.
Le tribunal se constitue dans les flammes,
la foule gonfle et ronfle, alimente le feu,
la foule a pris parmi le bois du sacrifice.
Qui est tenu sur le bûcher? La vieille
qui nous a porté un sort toute la vie,
ou le héros étincelant dans la ténèbre?
Qui maudit ou proclame? De qui l'odeur?
Je ne distingue pas la face noircie par les fumées.
Nous terrifiera-t-elle encore, ou s'il nous sauve?
Qui brûle? Qui brûle et pleure...
Et se dissipe, et se ranime si je suis là,
s'efface, chante, *CAMPO DE' FIORI* partout au monde.

– Les incendies ne sont peut-être qu'une humeur
du soleil déclinant.

[XII]

I flee amid jeers,
round behind the hill where, bearing the crown,
they are preparing the triumph. I hear the muffled
drum-beats, and the steps being climbed.
The tall fountain leaps in bursts. Unmoving dogs
before each gateway all along the arcades,
showing their teeth...
Mingling with the arrivals whose numbers are growing,
scattering, I go on, drawn by the voice,
I turn, still they turn, come out on to the square.
The tribunal is forming in the flames,
the crowd bulges and buzzes, feeds the fire,
the crowd has caught among the wood for sacrifice.
Who is held at the stake? The old woman
who told our fortunes all our lives,
or the hero glittering in the dark?
Who curses or proclaims? Whose smell?
I cannot make out the face blackened by smoke.
Will she still terrify us, or what if he saves us?
Who is burning? Who is burning, weeping...
And dissipates, revives if I am there,
fades, sings, *CAMPO DE' FIORI* throughout the world.

– Perhaps the fires are nothing but a mood
of the declining sun.

[XIII]

Est-ce aujourd'hui?
Dans les quartiers l'on se souvient, on imagine
un caprice ancien du tyran. Parmi nous,
trois cent soixante et une des églises ont été murées,
qui seront ouvertes un siècle après
quelques longues journées, au moment du solstice,
pour que l'on sache ce qu'il en reste,
au sortir de l'ensevelissement,
du murmure des orfèvreries et des ailes d'ange
et du signe que tu fis apparaître au troisième pilier.
Alors à nouveau,
le recours au marmottement
et la patience des vieilles femmes sur les degrés.

... Si les ossements ont peu changé, ni la pierre
un peu plus pâle, des araignées
qui avaient tissé sur les autels, très bleus, légers,
comme des langes, de longtemps sont tombées en poudre,
et se défont les langes
à la rumeur des portes que pousse la foule.
Vieux défunts sont les vers dans les retables taraudés!
Et les légendes se sont affaissées dans leur dorure,
entraînant l'ancien geste triomphal.

D'une grotte encastrée sur les toits,
par l'œil-de-bœuf qu'on a débouché,
du petit lit de fer,
si l'on voit s'allumer en tâtonnant
l'huile nouvelle dans les lampes,
quelle mémoire ancienne saurait reconnaître
les erreurs commises aux célébrations,
formule mal à propos, décalage dans les cortèges,
ricanement des cryptes, un jeune ange
adoré en place de la vierge, du sang apparu
dans les coquilles, ce bébé mort?

[XIII]

Is it today?
The locals remember, imagine
an ancient whim of the tyrant. Among us,
three hundred and sixty-one of the churches have been walled up,
which will be open a century later
for a few long days, at the moment of the solstice,
so that we know what is left of them,
as we come from the burial,
of the hum of goldsmiths' shops and angel-wings
and the sign you conjured up at the third pillar.
Then again,
the resort to muttering
and the patience of the old women on the steps.

...If the bones are little changed, nor the stone
a little paler, spiders
that had spun webs on the altars, very blue, light,
like swaddling-bands, long since have fallen to dust,
and the bands unwind
to the hubbub of the gates the crowd is pushing.
Old men deceased are the worms in the drilled altar-pieces!
And the legends have collapsed in their gildings,
dragging with them the old gesture of triumph.

From an embedded cave on the roofs,
through the bull's-eye window just unblocked,
from the small iron bed,
if we see the new oil in the lamps
struggling alight,
what ancient memory might recognise
the errors committed at celebrations,
an unsuitable form of words, processions out of step,
a cackling of crypts, a young angel
adored in place of the virgin, blood appearing
in shells, that baby dead?

Basta! Il est trop tard pour larmoyer, camarades.
Ce matin des milliers d'enfants
ont déjà défilé en pleurs en vain,
qui étaient venus portant des palmes.
Retour à l'origine. Un ventre vide,
voilà le secret. Ô mon Seigneur, sauve qui peut!

Basta! It's too late to snivel, comrades.
This morning thousands of children
have already filed past in tears in vain,
they'd come bearing palms.
Back to square one. An empty belly,
that's the secret. O my Lord, everyone for himself!

[XIV]

– Tous les œufs se fendaient pour qu'en sorte
un museau qui se dandinait en avançant, qui mordait...

– En s'ouvrant, quel atome ouvrira
l'univers neuf? Le nouvel œuf.

Pied de marbre, avec lanière de marbre
du soldat conquérant du monde,
débris qu'inventait la bonhomie populaire,
oublié aujourd'hui dans les détritus.
Cosa nostra! Mince univers, notre marche poursuivant,
ruptures et retours, dimension rétrécie, tutto compreso,
finito, morte.

Qu'allons-nous faire de tous ces marbres taillés?
Ces vierges qui n'ont plus cours, ces colonnades et ces palais
qui n'en finissent pas d'occuper la place?
Mais déjà nous ne sommes plus
présents qu'à peine, ce sont d'autres
qui vaquent à leurs affaires, et nul
n'entend désormais
des figures qui avaient pour nous charme ambigu.

D'autres paroles seront machinées, se déchaînent.
De nouveaux masques, on n'y retrouvera plus rien...
– On, c'est façon de dire, si nous sommes morts!
Le lierre fourmille, il agrippe un nouvel âge.
D'autres reconnaîtront
la fureur et les charmes, les emblèmes
de leur aujourd'hui.

– À leur tour, ils ne s'y reconnaissent pas.

[XIV]

– All the eggs cracked to let out
a muzzle that swung as it came forward, bit...

– As it opens, which atom will open
the brand-new universe? The new egg.

Marble foot, with a marble thong
of the soldier conquering people,
rubble invented by popular good-nature,
forgotten today among the rubbish.
Cosa nostra! Mean universe, our forward march,
ruptures and returns, narrow dimension, tutto compreso,
finito, morte.

What are we to do with all that hewn marble?
Those virgins no longer legal tender, those colonnades and palaces
forever taking up space?
But already we are
hardly there, while others
get on with their business, and no one
from now on understands
figures that had for us a two-edged charm.

Other words will be contrived, are breaking loose.
New masks, we'll get nothing more out of them...
– We, a fat lot that means, if we're dead!
The ivy swarms, it clutches a new age.
Others will recognise
fury and charms, the emblems
of their today.

– *It's their turn not to see themselves in them.*

[XV]

…Descendus des murs saints, les troupeaux en tumulte
sont passés par les rues vers le ravin,
les yeux des béliers, rouges la nuit.
– Des jeunes gens sourient là-bas, ils s'embrassent.
– De forts ânes montent les marches, le fardeau
bute sur la colonne, il tombe.
– La louve tarpéienne bâille entre les rochers.

Depuis toujours, par les excavations,
des couples de bergers
surgissent de la nuit la plus longue.
Avec la flûte et la cornemuse,
ils s'en vont par les guirlandes illuminées
pour annoncer encore un coup
l'antique naissance.

– Depuis trop longtemps se préparaient les captifs.

Des ribambelles de statues mutinées, de palais pris.
Des ritournelles pour enchanter les enfants pauvres,
pleurant qui rient.

Qui peut promettre ou compromettre ou conjurer?
Qui jugera?

Dans le sang caillé des morts ou des vivants,
qui lira les présages?
Ô très antique sibylle, ô vestale,
bouche de vérité si le cloaque fume!

ROME. PARIS. ROME.
Décembre 1963. Décembre 1969.

114

[XV]

...Down from the holy walls, the flocks have passed
helter-skelter through the streets towards the gully,
the rams' eyes red by night.
– Young people laugh down there, they kiss.
– Strong asses climb the steps, the burden
knocks against the column, it falls off.
– The Tarpeian she-wolf yawns between the rocks.

Always, during excavations,
shepherd couples
have come into view from the longest night.
With flute and bagpipes,
they go off by the lighted wreaths
to announce once again
the ancient birth.

For too long the captives had been prepared.

Strings of rebellious statues, of palaces captured.
Refrains to charm the children of the poor,
laughing as they weep.

Who can promise or compromise or ward off?
Who will judge?

From the congealed blood of the dead or the living,
who will read the omens?
O most ancient sibyl, O vestal virgin,
mouthpiece of truth above the steaming sewer!

ROME. PARIS. ROME.
December 1963. December 1969.

Bloodaxe Contemporary French Poets

Series Editors: Timothy Mathews & Michael Worton

FRENCH-ENGLISH BILINGUAL EDITIONS

1: **Yves Bonnefoy:** *On the Motion and Immobility óf Douve / Du mouvement et de l'immobilité de Douve*
Translated by Galway Kinnell. Introduction by Timothy Mathews.

2: **René Char:** *The Dawn Breakers / Les Matinaux*
Translated & introduced by Michael Worton.

3: **Henri Michaux:** *Spaced, Displaced / Déplacements Dégagements*
Translated by David & Helen Constantine. Introduction by Peter Broome.

4: **Aimé Césaire:** *Notebook of a Return to My Native Land / Cahier d'un retour au pays natal*
Translated by Mireille Rosello with Annie Pritchard.
Introduction by Mireille Rosello.

5: **Philippe Jaccottet:** *Under Clouded Skies / Beauregard Pensées sous les nuages / Beauregard*
Translated by David Constantine & Mark Treharne.
Introduction by Mark Treharne.

6: **Paul Éluard:** *Unbroken Poetry II / Poésie ininterrompue II*
Translated by Gilbert Bowen.
Introduction by Jill Lewis.

7: **André Frénaud:** Rome the Sorceress / *La Sorcière de Rome*
Translated by Keith Bosley.
Introduction by Peter Broome.

FORTHCOMING:

8: **Anne Hébert:** *The Tomb of the Kings / Le tombeau des rois*
Translated by Joanne Collie & Anne Hébert.
Introduction by Joanne Collie.

Other books planned for the series include works by Jacques Dupin, Guillevic, Pierre Jean Jouve, Gérard Macé, Jacques Roubaud, Gisèle Prassinos, Michel Deguy, Bernard Noël, Jacques Réda.

'Bloodaxe's Contemporary French Poets series could not have arrived at a more opportune time, and I cannot remember any translation initiative in the past thirty years that has been more ambitious or more coherently planned in its attempt to bring French poetry across the Channel and the Atlantic. Under the editorship of Timothy Mathews and Michael Worton, the series has a clear format and an even clearer sense of mission' – MALCOLM BOWIE, *The Times Literary Supplement*

YVES BONNEFOY
On the Motion and Immobility of Douve:
Du mouvement et de l'immobilité de Douve
Translated by Galway Kinnell. Introduction by Timothy Mathews.

Yves Bonnefoy is a central figure in post-war French culture. Born in 1923, he has had a lifelong fascination with the problems of translation. Language, for him, is a visceral, intensely material element in our existence, and yet the abstract quality of words distorts the immediate, material quality of our contact with the world.

This concern with what separates words from an essential truth hidden in objects involves him in wide-ranging philosophical and theological investigations of the spiritual and the sacred. But for all his intellectual drive and rigour, Bonnefoy's poetry is essentially of the concrete and the tangible, and addresses itself to our most familiar and intimate experiences of objects and of each other.

In his first book of poetry, published in France in 1953, Bonnefoy reflects on the value and mechanism of language in a series of short variations on the life and death of a much loved woman, Douve. In his introduction, Timothy Mathews shows how Bonnefoy's poetics are enmeshed with his philosophical, religious and critical thought.

Galway Kinnell is one of America's leading poets. His *Selected Poems* (1982) won the National Book Award and the Pulitzer Prize.

RENÉ CHAR
The Dawn Breakers:
Les Matinaux
Edited & translated by Michael Worton

René Char (1907-88) is generally regarded as one of the most important modern French poets. Admired by Heidegger for the profundity of his poetic philosophy, he was also a hero of the French Resistance and in the 1960s a militant anti-nuclear protester.

Associated with the Surrealist movement for several years and a close friend of many painters – notably Braque, Giacometti and Picasso – he wrote poetry which miraculously, often challengingly, confronts the major 20th century moral, political and artistic concerns with a simplicity of vision and expression that owes much to the poet-philosophers of ancient Greece.

Les Matinaux (1947-49) is perhaps his greatest collection. Published after the War, it looks forward to a better and freer world, whilst also bearing the marks of a deep-seated hatred of all fascisms. It contains some of the most beautiful love poems ever written in French.

Michael Worton's translations convey the essence of Char's poetry (which says difficult things in a simple, traditional way), and his introduction suggests why Char is one of the vital voices of our age.

BLOODAXE CONTEMPORARY FRENCH POETS: 3
HENRI MICHAUX
Spaced, Displaced:
Déplacements Dégagements
Translated by David & Helen Constantine. Introduction by Peter Broome.

Henri Michaux (1899-1984) is one of the notable travellers of modern French poetry: not only to the Amazon and the Far East, but into the strange hinterland of his own inner space, the surprises and shocks of which he has never ceased to explore as a foreign country in their own right, and a language to be learned. Fired by the same explorer's appetite, he has delved into the realm of mescaline and other drugs, and his wartime poetry, part of a private "resistance" movement of extraordinary density and energy, has advertised his view of the poetic act as a form of exorcism.

His insatiable thirst for new artistic expressions of himself made him one of the most aggressive and disquieting of contemporary French painters. If he is close to anyone, it is to Klee and Pollock, but he was as much inspired by Oriental graphic arts.

Déplacements Dégagements (1985) has all the hallmarks of Michaux's most dynamic work: poetry testing itself dangerously at the frontiers, acutely analytical, linguistically versatile and full of surprising insights into previously undiscovered movements of the mind.

David Constantine is Fellow in German at the Queen's College, Oxford. He has published five books of poems and a novel with Bloodaxe, and has translated poetry from French, Greek and German. Helen Constantine has taught French at schools and polytechnics in Durham and Oxford. Peter Broome is Professor of French at Queen's University, Belfast. He is co-author of *The Appreciation of Modern French Poetry* and *An Anthology of Modern French Poetry* (CUP, 1976), and author of monographs on Michaux and Frénaud.

AIMÉ CÉSAIRE

Notebook of a Return to My Native Land:
Cahier d'un retour au pays natal

Translated by Mireille Rosello with Annie Pritchard.
Introduction by Mireille Rosello.

André Breton called Aimé Césaire's *Cahier* 'nothing less than the greatest lyrical monument of this time'. It is a seminal text in Surrealist, French and Black literatures, only now published in full in English for the first time.

Aimé Césaire was born in 1913 in Basse-Pointe, a village on the north coast of Martinique, a former French colony in the Caribbean (now an overseas département of France). His *Notebook of a Return to My Native Land* is the foundation stone of francophone Black literature: it is here that the word *Negritude* appeared for the first time. *Negritude* has come to mean the cultural, philosophical and political movement co-founded in Paris in the 1930s by three Black students from French colonies: the poets Léon-Gontran Damas from French Guiana; Léopold Senghor, later President of Senegal; and Aimé Césaire, who became a deputy in the French National Assembly for the Revolutionary Party of Martinique and was until very recently Mayor of Fort-de-France.

As a poet, Césaire believes in the revolutionary power of language, and in the *Notebook* he combines high literary French with Martinican colloquialisms, and archaic turns of phrase with dazzling new coinages. The result is a challenging and deeply moving poem on the theme of the future of the negro race which presents and enacts the poignant search for a Martinican identity. The *Notebook* opposes the ideology of colonialism by inventing a language that refuses assimilation to a dominant cultural norm, a language that teaches resistance and liberation.

Mireille Rosello lectures in French at the University of Southampton. Her books, all in French, include *Littérature et identité créole aux Antilles*, and studies of André Breton and Michel Tournier.

'Aimé Césaire's *Notebook of a Return to My Native Land* is one of the most extraordinary written this century... *Notebook* is a declaration of independence...As ambitious as Joyce, Césaire sets out to "forge the uncreated conscience" of his race...Rosello's introduction discusses the poem's influence on later Caribbean writers, many of whom have sought to close the gap between the literary and the vernacular that *Notebook* so vividly explores' – MARK FORD, *Guardian*

PHILIPPE JACCOTTET

Under Clouded Skies / Beauregard
Pensées sous les nuages / Beauregard

Translated by Mark Treharne & David Constantine.
Introduction by Mark Treharne.
Poetry Book Society Recommended Translation

Philippe Jaccottet's poetry is meditative, immediate and sensuous. It is rooted in the Drôme region of south-east France, which gives it a rich sense of place. This book brings together his reflections on landscape in the prose pieces of *Beauregard* (1981) and in the poems of *Under Clouded Skies* (1983), two thematically linked collections which are remarkable for their lyrical restraint and quiet power.

Jaccottet's poetry is largely grounded in landscape and the visual world, pursuing an anxious and persistent questioning of natural signs, meticulously conveyed in a syntax of great inventiveness. His work is animated by a fascination with the visible world from which he translates visual objects into verbal images and ultimately into figures of language. His poems are highly attentive, pushing the eye beyond what it sees, enacting a rich hesitation between meaning conferred and meaning withheld.

Born in Switzerland in 1925, Philippe Jaccottet is one of the most prominent figures of the immediate post-war generation of French poets. He has lived in France since 1953, working as a translator and freelance writer. As well as poetry, he has published prose writings, notebooks and critical essays. He is particularly well-known as a translator from German (Musil, Rilke, Mann, Hölderlin) but has also translated Homer, Plato, Ungaretti, Montale, Góngora and Mandelstam. He has won many distinguished prizes for his work both in France and elsewhere. His *Selected Poems*, translated by Derek Mahon, was published by Penguin in 1988.

Mark Treharne taught French at the University of Warwick until 1992. He has translated much of Jaccottet's prose and written on modern French Literature. **David Constantine** is Fellow in German at the Queen's College, Oxford. He has published five books of poems and a novel with Bloodaxe, and has translated poetry from French, Greek and German. The translators worked in close collaboration with Philippe Jaccottet on this edition.

BLOODAXE CONTEMPORARY FRENCH POETS: 6

PAUL ÉLUARD
Unbroken Poetry II
Poésie ininterrompue II
Translated by Gilbert Bowen.
Introduction by Jill Lewis.

Paul Éluard's poetry is concerned with sexual desire and the desire for social change. A central participant in Dada and in the Surrealist movement, Éluard joined the French Communist Party and worked actively in the Resistance in Nazi-occupied Paris. Caught between the horrors of Stalinism and post-war, right-wing anti-communism, his writing sustains an insistent vision of poetry as a multi-faceted weapon against injustice and oppression. For Éluard, poetry is a way of infiltrating the reader with greater emotional awareness of the social problems of the modern world.

Unbroken Poetry II, published posthumously in 1953, pays tribute to Dominique Éluard, with whom Paul spent the last years of his life. It traces the internal dialogues of a passionate relationship as well as of his continuing re-evaluation of the poetic project itself. It centres on political commitment and places it at the heart of the lovers' desire.

After completing a successful business career, **Gilbert Bowen** embarked on his first volume of translated work, *Paul Éluard: Selected Poems* (John Calder, 1987). This was followed by translations of work by Jacques Prévert and of writers from French-speaking Africa. His poetry has appeared in various magazines.

Jill Lewis is Associate Professor of Literature and Feminist Studies at Hampshire College, Amherst, Massachusetts. She is co-author of *Common Differences: conflicts in black and white feminist perspectives*, and is currently completing a book on Paul Éluard entitled *Of Politics and Desire*. Since 1989, her work on cultural studies, gender and sexuality has involved her strongly in AIDS-related work.

Other French Editions from Bloodaxe

JACQUES DUPIN
Selected Poems
Translated by Paul Auster, Stephen Romer & David Shapiro

Jacques Dupin was born in 1927 in Privas in the Ardèche. Images of the harsh mineral nakedness of his native countryside run through the whole of his work and figure a fundamental existential nakedness. Dupin is an ascetic who likes the bare and the simple. His poetry is sad, wise and relentlessly honest. He speaks in our ear, as if at once close and far off, to tell us what we knew: 'Neither passion nor possession'.

He is a poet and art critic, and a formidable authority on the work of Miró and Giacometti. This edition of his prose poems and lyrics has been selected by Paul Auster from seven collections published between 1958 and 1982, culminating in his *Songs of Rescue*. It has an introduction by Mary Ann Caws, Professor of French at City University of New York.

PIERRE REVERDY
Selected Poems
Translated by John Ashbery, Mary Ann Caws & Patricia Terry
Edited by Timothy Bent & Germaine Brée

Pierre Reverdy (1889-1960) is one of the greatest and most influential figures in modern French poetry. He founded the journal *Nord-Sud* with Max Jacob and Guillaume Apollinaire, which drew together the first Surrealists. Associated with painters such as Picasso, Gris and Braque, he has been called a Cubist poet, for conventional structure is eliminated in his *poésie brut* ('raw poetry'), much as the painters cut away surface appearance to bring through the underlying forms. But Reverdy went beyond Cubist desolation to express a profound spiritual doubt and his sense of a mystery in the universe forever beyond his understanding.

André Breton hailed him in the first Surrealist Manifesto as 'the greatest poet of the time'. Louis Aragon said that for Breton, Soupault, Éluard and himself, Reverdy was 'our immediate elder, the exemplary poet'.

JEAN TARDIEU
The River Underground:
Selected Poems & Prose
Translated by David Kelley

The poetry of **Jean Tardieu** (1903-95) has an almost child-like simplicity, and in France his work is studied both in universities and in primary schools. Yet while he was a household name in France and has been translated into most European languages, his poetry remains little known in the English-speaking world, despite its immediacy and sense of fun.

In his early years the difficulties of writing lyric poetry in a schizophrenic age led Tardieu to a multiplication of poetic voices, and so to working for the stage, and he was writing what was subsequently dubbed 'Theatre of the Absurd' before Beckett's and Ionesco's plays had ever been performed.

This selection includes the sequence *Space and the Flute* (1958), which Tardieu wrote for drawings by his friend Pablo Picasso. Their poems and drawings are reproduced together in this edition, which spans 80 years of Tardieu's writing.

ALISTAIR ELLIOT
French Love Poems
Poetry Book Society Recommended Translation

French Love Poems is about the kinds of love that puzzle, delight and afflict us throughout our lives, from going on walks with an attractive cousin before Sunday dinner (Nerval) to indulging a granddaughter (Hugo). On the way there's the first yes from lips we love (Verlaine), a sky full of stars reflected fatally in Cleopatra's eyes (Heredia), lying awake waiting for your lover (Valéry), and the defeated toys of dead children (Gautier).

The selection covers five centuries, from Ronsard to Valéry. Other poets represented include Baudelaire, Mallarmé, Rimbaud, La Fontaine, Laforgue and Leconte de Lisle. The 35 poems, chosen by Alistair Elliot, are printed opposite his own highly skilful verse translations. There are also helpful notes on French verse technique and on points of obscurity.

THE NEW FRENCH POETRY
Edited & translated by
David Kelley & Jean Khalfa

This anthology captures the excitement of one of the most chal-
lenging developments in contemporary French writing, the new
metaphysical poetry which has become an influential strand in
recent French literature. It is a rigorously ontological poetry con-
cerned with the very being of things, and with the nature of poetic
language itself.

This is not the only kind of poetry being written in France
today, but it is an extremely significant development, not only in
French poetry, but also in French writing as a whole. Indeed, some
of the writers included in this book, notably Édmond Jabès and
Gérard Macé, have been influential in the subversion of conventional
genres, by the play between poetry, narrative and essay, which has
been an important aspect of recent French literature.

This anthology brings together writers of difference generations,
from Gisèle Prassinos and Joyce Mansour, through Jacques Dupin
and Bernard Noël, to Frank-André Jamme and André Velter. It
represents those who are major figures in France and already have
some reputation in Britain and America, alongside writers who are
still relatively unknown to English readers. Much of the poetry
shows an affinity with the work of Henri Michaux. The book also
reflects the range of poetry published by the innovative French
imprint Éditions Fata Morgana, as well as the lists of leading French
publishers such as Gallimard, Éditions du Seuil and Mercure de
France.

David Kelley is Senior Lecturer in French and Director of
Studies in Modern Languages at Trinity College, Cambridge. His
books include his edition *The River Underground: Selected Poems
& Prose* by Jean Tardieu (Bloodaxe Books, 1991), and a translation
of Gérard Macé forthcoming in the Bloodaxe Contemporary
French Poets series. **Jean Khalfa** is a distinguished French scholar
and a former diplomat. He is currently a Fellow of Trinity College,
Cambridge.

PAUL VALÉRY
La Jeune Parque
Translated by Alistair Elliot

'A poem should not mean, but be,' said Archibald MacLeish. *La Jeune Parque* ('the goddess of Fate as a young woman') certainly exists: she's beautiful and makes great gestures. And as for what she means, there's a substantial amount of argument about that, so *La Jeune Parque* is a poem by either definition. It's a classic, by general agreement, written to the full 17th-century recipe for alexandrine couplets, and it's modern, with every word pulling its weight in more than one direction.

Alistair Elliot's parallel translation with notes is aimed at making this rewarding but difficult long poem accessible enough for bafflement to turn into admiration. He attempts to clarify its small puzzles and also trace the overall narrative line of Paul Valéry's poem: it does have a story (what should a young woman do?) and does struggle towards a resolution. He also provides an introduction which deals with the interesting circumstances of the poem's four-year composition (1913-17), which resulted in Valery's instantly becoming a famous poet at the age of forty-five, after having written no poetry for twenty years.

This is Alistair Elliot's fifth book of verse translation – the others being Verlaine's *Femmes/Hombres* (Anvil), Heine's *The Lazarus Poems* (MidNAG/Carcanet), and *French Love Poems* and *Italian Landscape Poems* (both Bloodaxe). He has also edited a parallel-text version of Virgil's *Georgics* with Dryden's translation (MidNAG), and translated Euripides' *Medea*, the basis of Diana Rigg's prize-winning performances at the Almeida Theatre (1992) and elsewhere. His own Collected Poems, *My Country* (1989), and his latest collection, *Turning the Stones* (1993), are published by Carcanet.